AS/A Level

King Lear

William Shakespeare

**Oxford
Literature
Companions**

Notes and activities: Carmel Waldron
Series consultant: Peter Buckroyd

OXFORD
UNIVERSITY PRESS

Contents

Language 54

Themes 66

Performance 78

Critical Views 86

Skills and Practice 98

Glossary and Further Reading 118

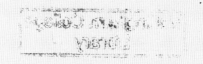

What are Oxford Literature Companions?

Oxford Literature Companions is a series designed to provide you with comprehensive support for popular set texts. You can use the Companion alongside your play, using relevant sections during your studies or using the book as a whole for revision.

Each Companion includes detailed guidance and practical activities on:

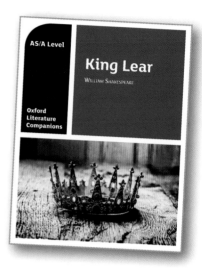

- Plot and Structure
- Context
- Genre
- Characterization and Roles
- Language
- Themes
- Performance
- Critical Views
- Skills and Practice

How does this book help with exam preparation?

As well as providing guidance on key areas of the play, throughout this book you will also find 'Upgrade' features. These are tips to help with your exam preparation and performance.

In addition, in the extensive **Skills and Practice** chapter, the 'Exam skills' section provides detailed guidance on areas such as how to prepare for the exam, understanding the question, planning your response and hints for what to do (or not do) in the exam.

In the **Skills and Practice** chapter there is also a bank of **Sample questions** and **Sample answers**. The **Sample answers** are marked and include annotations and a summative comment.

How does this book help with terminology?

Throughout the book, key terms are highlighted in the text and explained on the same page. There is also a detailed **Glossary** at the end of the book that explains, in the context of the play, all the relevant literary terms highlighted in this book.

Which edition of the play has this book used?

Quotations and character names have been taken from the Oxford School Shakespeare edition of *King Lear* (ISBN 978-0-19-839222-4).

How does this book work?

Each book in the Oxford Literature Companions series follows the same approach and includes the following features:

- **Key quotations** from the play
- **Key terms** explained on the page and linked to a complete glossary at the end of the book
- **Activity boxes** to help improve your understanding of the text
- **Upgrade** tips to help prepare you for your assessment

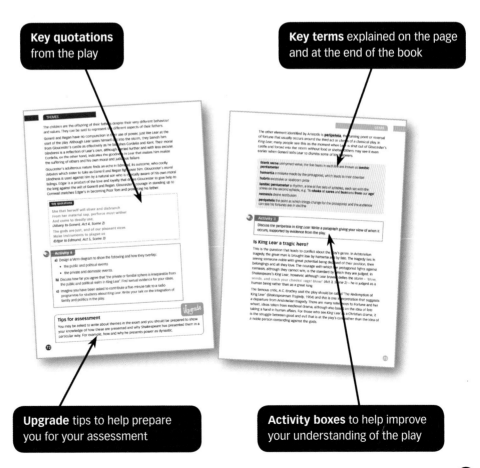

Key quotations from the play

Key terms explained on the page and at the end of the book

Upgrade tips to help prepare you for your assessment

Activity boxes to help improve your understanding of the play

Plot and Structure

Plot

Act 1, Scene 1

The play opens with a conversation between the Earl of Kent and the Earl of Gloucester, which introduces the division of the kingdom.

King Lear enters with his court and announces his intention of dividing the kingdom into three and giving these lands as his daughters' dowries. He intends to give up rule and responsibility, while retaining 'The name and all th'addition to a king'. But, as a test, his daughters must first tell him how much they love him. Goneril and Regan make flattering speeches declaring their boundless love and receive their portions. Cordelia says only that she loves Lear as a daughter should love a father. He flies into a rage at her refusal to flatter him and disowns her. He then banishes Kent for telling him how unwise he is. The King of France is filled with admiration for Cordelia and gladly accepts her as his wife.

- The theme of fathers and children is introduced in the two families of Lear and his daughters, and Gloucester and his sons.
- The idea of division is made clear, both with the physical splitting of the country and the contrast between Cordelia and her sisters, as well as the rift between Lear and Cordelia.
- The character flaws in Lear are shown as he demands obedience and is seen to value flattery above plain speaking. His rashness in disowning Cordelia and banishing Kent sow the seeds of his downfall.
- Gloucester is shown as lacking in morality and sensitivity when he boasts of how Edmund was conceived.

In dividing his kingdom, Lear reveals his flaws – vanity and rashness, lack of knowledge of himself and his children. This image is from Trevor Nunn's production of *King Lear,* 2009

Activity 1

Discuss the behaviour of Lear in this scene and predict what you think will be the result of:

- his division of the kingdom while wanting to retain power
- his banishment of Cordelia
- his banishment of Kent.

Act 1, Scene 2

Edmund enters. In his **soliloquy**, he questions why he should be treated as a bastard and announces his intention to take land from 'Legitimate Edgar'. He shows a letter, which he pretends to put away in haste as Gloucester enters. The letter suggests that Edgar is plotting his father's death and offering Edmund half his inheritance to help him. Gloucester demands to see the letter and believes the plot. Edmund then informs Edgar that somebody has told lies to his father about him and warns him to be careful and to go armed.

- This scene reveals Edmund's true character and motives to the audience.
- Edmund's duplicity mirrors that of Goneril and Regan, in different circumstances.
- This scene reveals the flaws in Gloucester's character as he does not seem to understand his sons and believes Edmund instead of Edgar.
- It shows the audience the differences between the two brothers.

> **soliloquy** a speech delivered by a character when they are, or believe they are, alone on stage

Act 1, Scene 3

Goneril is already tired of Lear behaving as if he still ruled and tells her steward Oswald to treat Lear discourteously so that he will leave and go to Regan, who feels as she does.

- The audience is shown Goneril's true nature as she tries to provoke Lear into a quarrel.
- The close relationship between Goneril and her steward Oswald is apparent.

Act 1, Scene 4

Kent enters in disguise and asks Lear if he can serve him. He defends the king when Oswald is rude towards him. Goneril rounds on Lear and claims his knights are turning her house into 'a riotous inn' and she insists he must get rid of half his followers. Lear is furious and decides to go to Regan. He curses Goneril and leaves. Goneril sends Oswald with a letter to Regan to warn her of Lear's impending arrival.

- This scene shows the contrast between the loyalty of Kent and the ingratitude of Goneril.
- Lear's behaviour is shown to be rash and changeable.
- The wisdom of the Fool, who sees Goneril and Regan for what they are, becomes apparent.

Act 1, Scene 5

Lear sends the disguised Kent with a letter to Regan, announcing his intention to stay with her.

Act 2, Scene 1

At Gloucester's house, Edmund learns there are rumours of civil war and that Regan and her husband the Duke of Cornwall are expected shortly. He warns Edgar he must run away, as Gloucester has ordered his arrest. He stages a fight and wounds himself to give his story against Edgar more credibility. When Regan arrives, she says she left home as she heard that Lear was on his way with his unruly train.

- This scene shows the lengths to which Edmund will go against his brother.
- It shows that Regan will behave in the same way as Goneril.

Act 2, Scene 2

Oswald arrives at the same time as the disguised Kent, who accuses him of working against Lear. They quarrel violently, which results in Cornwall putting Kent in the stocks. Kent reads a letter from Cordelia that implies she has heard about the state of things and will somehow remedy them.

- This scene reveals how little respect Regan and Cornwall show for Lear.
- It shows Kent has remained in touch with Cordelia.

Act 2, Scene 3

Edgar announces his intention to disguise himself as 'Poor Tom', a bedlam beggar, to avoid capture and death.

Bedlam beggars

In Shakespeare's day, the name 'Tom o' Bedlam' was often used for beggars who either had or pretended to have mental illness. In fact, a popular poem called 'Tom o'Bedlam' was written around the beginning of the 17th century, giving a 'voice' to a so-called homeless 'Bedlamite'. The association with 'Bedlam' came about because people thought that these beggars had been released from the Bethlem Royal Hospital in London.

Act 2, Scene 4

Lear arrives at Gloucester's castle and is astonished to find Kent in the stocks. Kent tells him that no sooner had he given Lear's letter to Regan than Oswald arrived with a letter from Goneril, which made Regan and Cornwall depart in haste. When Lear demands their attendance, Regan and Cornwall send excuses until Lear threatens to break down their doors.

When Regan and Cornwall finally appear, Kent is freed and Regan makes it clear she is on her sister's side. She bids Lear return to Goneril, who arrives just then at Gloucester's castle.

Seeing how powerless he has made himself, in rage and frustration, Lear leaves the castle and goes out into the storm. Cornwall tells Gloucester to shut his doors.

- This scene provides the climactic action as Lear is shut out in the storm with only the Fool for company.
- The audience is made aware of the lengths to which Goneril and Regan will go to undermine their father.
- The ultimate result of Lear's initial rash decision is seen in his rapid descent from all-powerful monarch to homeless old man.

> **Key quotation**
>
> O, reason not the need! our basest beggars
> Are in the poorest thing superfluous:
> Allow not nature more than nature needs,
> Man's life is cheap as beast's.
> (Lear, Act 2, Scene 4)

Activity 2

Design a bar chart or graph showing how the balance of power between Lear and his daughters changes throughout the first two acts. You will need to define the events which show these changes.

Act 3, Scene 1

Kent tells Lear's gentleman that the French army is waiting for a chance to invade and asks him to go to Dover, find Cordelia and give her a ring. They both exit, looking for Lear.

- This short scene tells the audience that Cordelia has landed in Britain and gives hope for Lear's relief.

Act 3, Scene 2

Lear enters with the Fool, defying the storm and all the elements 'I never gave you kingdom, call'd you children'. Kent enters and tells Lear that there is a hovel nearby that will provide shelter, and he exits with Lear and the Fool.

- Lear is shown defying the elements that rage overhead, preferring them to his own daughters.
- The Fool reminds Lear of his folly, even as he tries to persuade him to seek shelter.

> **Key quotation**
>
> Blow, winds, and crack your cheeks! rage! blow!
> (Lear, Act 3, Scene 2)

Act 3, Scene 3

Gloucester confides to Edmund that he has been forbidden to help Lear and that he has a secret, and dangerous, letter. He says he is going to find Lear.

Act 3, Scene 4

Lear, Kent and the Fool discover Edgar, disguised as Poor Tom in the hovel. Lear is convinced his 'pelican daughters' must have brought him to this pass. He is losing his mind and believes that Poor Tom is a wise philosopher. Gloucester enters with a torch and finally persuades Lear to go inside. He tells Kent that Lear's daughters 'seek his death'.

Lear thinks that Poor Tom is a wise philosopher, the Old Vic, London, 2003

- In this scene the main plot and subplot join in the theme of madness.
- Lear seems to find some meaning in Poor Tom's ravings, which implies he is losing his grip on reality.
- Gloucester is shown to be willing to risk death to help Lear.

Act 3, Scene 5

Edmund betrays his father to Cornwall over the secret letter from France and Cornwall promises to make him Earl of Gloucester when his father is arrested for treason.

- This short scene reveals the depths of Edmund's betrayal and Cornwall's cynical abuse of power.

Act 3, Scene 6

Gloucester leaves Lear, Edgar, Kent and the Fool in a farmhouse near his castle, where Lear arranges a mock trial of his daughters. Gloucester enters and tells Kent to take Lear urgently to Dover because his two elder daughters are planning his murder.

- This scene demonstrates how far Lear has descended into madness.
- It also shows how much truth there can be in madness.

> **Key quotation**
>
> He childed as I father'd!
> (Edgar, Act 3, Scene 6)

Act 3, Scene 7

Back inside Gloucester's castle, Cornwall tells Regan to 'Post speedily to my lord your husband' with Edmund's escort and tell him that the French army has landed. Gloucester is brought in and tied to a chair. He is accused of treason and Cornwall, encouraged by Regan, destroys one of his eyes. One of the servants is so angered that he draws a sword to stop Cornwall and they fight. Regan takes a sword and stabs the servant in the back. Cornwall gouges out Gloucester's other eye and, when Gloucester calls for Edmund, Regan tells him it was Edmund who betrayed him.

Gloucester realizes he has been deceived and that Edgar is his loyal son. He is turned out of his castle to find his way to Dover. Cornwall is wounded and calls for Regan's help, while the other servants prepare to take care of Gloucester and ask Poor Tom to guide him.

- This brutal scene shows the cruelty of Cornwall and Regan.
- The theme of blindness is given physical shape in this scene.

> **Key quotation**
>
> Go thrust him out at gates, and let him smell
> His way to Dover.
> (Regan, Act 3, Scene 7)

Act 4, Scene 1

The blinded Gloucester meets Edgar, as Poor Tom, who volunteers to lead him to Dover, where Gloucester wishes to throw himself from a cliff.

> **Key quotation**
>
> As flies to wanton boys, are we to th'gods;
> They kill us for their sport.
> (Gloucester, Act 4, Scene 1)

Act 4, Scene 2

Meanwhile Goneril arrives home accompanied by Edmund. When she learns from Oswald that Albany is behaving oddly over the French invasion, she sends Edmund back, with a kiss, to rouse Cornwall to arms. Albany quarrels with Goneril, calling her a fiend for her treatment of Lear. A messenger tells them of Gloucester's blinding and Cornwall's death. Goneril's first thought is that Regan is now free to marry Edmund.

- The jealousy between the sisters brings a new division between them as well as between Goneril and Albany.
- This scene shows Albany in a new light and he has a more important role from now on.

> **Key quotation**
>
> Wisdom and goodness to the vile seem vile;
> Filths savour but themselves.
> (Albany, Act 4, Scene 2)

Act 4, Scene 3

Kent discovers that Lear has not met Cordelia, for 'burning shame / Detains him from Cordelia'.

- This scene reports on Cordelia's reaction to her sisters' treatment of their father.
- It also tells of Lear's repentance and shame of his treatment of Cordelia.

Act 4, Scenes 4 and 5

Cordelia asks for a doctor's help with Lear and sends her knights to find him.

Regan tells Oswald that, as a widow, she is free to marry Edmund. She further charges him to kill Gloucester, which Oswald promises to do.

- This scene develops the rivalry between the sisters over Edmund.
- It also shows that Gloucester's life is in danger.

Act 4, Scene 6

Edgar leads Gloucester to what he says is a high cliff, and the old man falls. Edgar then pretends to be a local peasant and tells Gloucester he was miraculously saved. Gloucester believes him and interprets his survival as a sign that he should bear his ills patiently.

Then Lear enters, wearing a crown of weeds and clearly out of his senses. Gloucester and Lear finally recognize each other. However, when Cordelia's attendants try to take Lear, he runs off.

Oswald enters and announces his intention of killing Gloucester. Edgar kills Oswald instead and reads the letter from Goneril, which talks of 'A plot upon her virtuous husband's life, / And the exchange my brother!' (Act 4, Scene 6).

- This scene develops the theme of patience and suffering.
- It shows Edgar's true nature.
- The meeting of Lear and Gloucester brings together the two repentant fathers, one blind and the other mad.

Act 4, Scene 7

Lear awakes in his right mind and is finally reconciled with Cordelia.

- This scene brings reconciliation and a kind of closure to part of the main plot.

Act 5, Scene 1

Regan shows her jealousy over Edmund, while Edgar appears and, giving Goneril's letter to Albany, says he will be his champion.

- This scene further develops the sisters' rivalry over Edmund and Edmund's ambition to take the crown.
- It shows Albany as trusted, even though he fights against Cordelia.
- It suggests that Edgar will finally throw off his disguise.

Act 5, Scene 2

Gloucester, left by Edgar, hears the sound of the battle, which is lost by Cordelia.

> **Key quotation**
>
> Men must endure
> Their going hence, even as their coming hither:
> Ripeness is all.
>
> *(Edgar, Act 5, Scene 2)*

Act 5, Scene 3

Edmund sends Lear and Cordelia to prison and Lear goes joyfully with his daughter. Edmund refuses to release them to Albany. Regan claims Edmund as husband, but is taken sick and helped to her tent.

The herald sounds the trumpet and Edgar appears, to challenge Edmund as a traitor. They fight and Edmund falls. Albany shows Goneril's letter to Edgar and Goneril rushes out. Edgar discloses his identity and tells how he guided his father and revealed who he was to his father, and that Gloucester died of joy.

King Lear Weeping over the Body of Dead Cordelia by James Barry, 1788

A messenger comes in to say that Goneril has committed suicide after poisoning Regan. Kent enters in search of Lear, and Edmund confesses that he has arranged for both Lear and Cordelia to be hanged. A messenger is sent to stop the hanging, but is too late.

Lear enters with the dead Cordelia in his arms. Kent reveals himself to Lear, but the king is too grieved to take notice of him or the deaths of his other daughters. Albany promises to restore the kingdom to Lear, and Edgar and Kent to their proper estates. The death of Edmund is greeted as a trifle.

Lear dies of a broken heart. Albany wants Edgar and Kent to rule the kingdom, but Kent says he must follow Lear into death. Edgar and Albany are left to restore the kingdom from the chaos.

- The final scene in the play sees the deaths of Regan, Goneril, Edmund, Gloucester, Cordelia and Lear.
- These deaths were all necessary, with the exception of Cordelia's, since these people were responsible for initiating and developing the trail of destruction.
- Lear dies of a broken heart, having found love rather than power, then losing it.

Activity 3

Design a timeline for *King Lear* that includes the main events of the plot, the locations of events and the significance of each event for the plot as a whole.

Structure

Five-act structure

Shakespeare's plays follow the rules laid down by Aristotle for the five-act structure: **exposition**, **rising action** (development), **climax**, **falling action**, and **denouement** (resolution).

The exposition in tragedy sets up the notion of conflict and sows the seeds for its development towards the final catastrophe and resolution. In *King Lear,* it is the idea of Lear dividing his kingdom in the main plot and Edmund's plan to cut Edgar off from his rightful inheritance in the subplot.

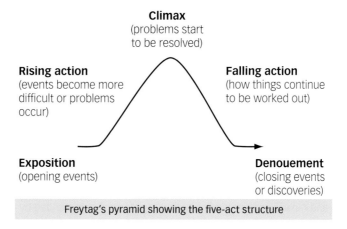

Climax
(problems start
to be resolved)

Rising action
(events become more
difficult or problems
occur)

Falling action
(how things continue
to be worked out)

Exposition
(opening events)

Denouement
(closing events
or discoveries)

Freytag's pyramid showing the five-act structure

Lear's action in the first scene is the first exposition; it is the inciting incident that triggers the rest of the plot. This scene shows Lear's flaws – his lack of knowledge of himself and his children, his vanity and rashness – which cause him to reject the one child who truly loves him and initiates the inevitable conflict that follows.

climax the point in a literary work in which the tension reaches its highest point

denouement the final part of the plot where all the loose ends are tied up

exposition introduction of events, settings and characters to the audience

falling action sequence of events after the climax but before the resolution

rising action series of incidents that create tension and interest for the audience

The second exposition is spread across Scenes 1 and 2 and concerns the subplot. Gloucester, like Lear, is shown to be lacking in perception of himself and his children. Edmund tells the audience he intends to discredit Edgar in his father's eyes and become Gloucester's heir. He prompts the action with the use of a letter, which arouses Gloucester's suspicion of Edgar and leads to the later tragedy.

The development stage begins in Act 1 with Goneril's refusal to put up with Lear's retinue any longer and her decision that he must **'disquantity your train'** (*Act 1, Scene 4*). Her treatment of him is thrown into relief by the loyalty of the banished Kent, and the conflict between Kent and Oswald mirrors that between Lear and Goneril. Lear's rage at being deprived of the remains of his power is inflamed by the realization that he has made a terrible mistake in trusting Goneril and he calls down a curse on her that mirrors his earlier rejection of Cordelia.

The development continues into Act 2 with Lear departing to stay with Regan. The subplot also develops in Act 2, as Edmund convinces Edgar that he must leave before he is arrested and then pretends to Gloucester that he was wounded in his father's defence. The rising action, which consists of the two sisters and Cornwall taking over Gloucester's castle and working hand in hand to deprive Lear of the last vestige of his authority, culminates in Lear being locked out in the middle of a storm.

At this climax in the play, there is a change as Lear is no longer able to influence events and the main action is driven by Goneril, Regan, Cornwall and Edmund. As the characters with the most power, they are in the ascendant. The conflict for Lear is now between sanity and madness, and he relies on Kent and Gloucester to look after him. The first intimations of conflict for the new rulers are the rumours of discord between Cornwall and Albany, and the landing of the French army commanded by Cordelia.

Edmund's betrayal of his father and Gloucester's subsequent blinding lead to Cornwall's death, the first blow to the hopes of the treacherous rulers.

In the falling action after this point, Albany makes clear his support for Lear, in a further division amongst the rulers. Edgar's discovery of Goneril's letter after he kills Oswald provides his opportunity to face his brother in combat, while the sisters' rivalry over Edmund leads to their deaths as well.

The denouement, in a cruel final twist, shows Edmund's repentance over his sentence on Lear and Cordelia coming too late. This bleak ending leaves little room for comfort.

Activity 4

Draw an outline of Freytag's pyramid and include what you see as the main events for each of the five stages – exposition, rising action, climax, falling action and denouement.

Double plot

The main plot, concerning Lear and his three daughters, is mirrored and complemented by the subplot, which follows Gloucester and his two sons. This structure gives depth and richness to the play because the audience can compare the relationships within and between the families. Lear's deception by the hypocrisy of Goneril and Regan is paralleled by Edmund's deception of Gloucester. Both Cordelia and Edgar, the children with genuine filial love, are made outcast for different reasons, while the deceived fathers blindly trust their treacherous siblings.

As the plot moves forward, the two families become more enmeshed. Gloucester's castle is the venue for Lear's final humiliation after which he too assumes the role of outcast. In this situation, he is helped by the other outcasts, Kent and Edgar, and accompanied only by his fool, a character who is set apart because of his job. After Gloucester's 'treason' in helping Lear, he too becomes an outcast, after being blinded, and is helped and guided by his outcast son, Edgar.

This pattern of outcast and replacement reinforces the ideas of division and suffering that lead to Lear's madness and Gloucester's blindness. The king, who acts irrationally, is punished with insanity while the earl, who lacks perception, is punished with blindness.

The main plot and subplot run parallel as Lear and Gloucester are brought down by the actions of Goneril, Regan and Edmund. Gert Voss plays Lear and Martin Schwab plays Gloucester in this production at Vienna's Burgtheater in 2007

Activity 5

Discuss all the similarities you can find between the plot and subplot, for example in the trial of Gloucester and the mock trial of the daughters.

Time scheme

The time scheme in *King Lear* is speedy. Once the kingdom is divided, its descent into chaos is rapid. Lear has barely departed from the stage before Goneril and Regan are plotting how to deal with his **'unruly waywardness'** and **'unconstant starts'** (*Act 1, Scene 1*). The next time we see Goneril, she is telling Oswald to be rude and careless in his approach to the king and his train in order to provoke a quarrel. A couple of days later, Lear has quarrelled with Goneril and by the end of Act 1 he's preparing to leave her and take up residence with Regan.

Act 2 begins with Edgar being forced to flee his home and become Poor Tom, while it appears that, not only are there strong rumours of a civil war between the dukes, but Cordelia is in touch with Kent and **'seeking to give / Losses their remedies'** (*Act 2, Scene 2*). By the end of Act 2, Lear has arrived at Gloucester's castle, quarrelled with Regan as well as Goneril and become an outcast in his own realm.

Act 3 sees Lear's rapid descent into madness while Cordelia has landed at Dover with the French army. Gloucester's knowledge of this and his kindness towards the king gives Edmund the opportunity he's been waiting for. While Kent, Edgar and the Fool take Lear to safety in Dover, Edmund's betrayal of Gloucester results in his blinding and ejection from his castle. The wounding of Cornwall during this event sets up the evil love triangle between Goneril, Regan and Edmund.

Act 4 sees Edgar guiding his blinded father to Dover and teaching him to bear the will of Fortune with patience. The divisions between Albany and Goneril, and Goneril and Regan grow wider even as they prepare their armies for battle. Lear is reunited first with Gloucester and then with Cordelia, and by the end of Act 4 it is the eve of the battle, Cornwall and Oswald are both dead and Lear has regained his sanity.

At the start of Act 5 all seems set for a possible happy ending and the action moves rapidly through scenes where Edgar presents his request for combat to Albany and the shortest battle ever, which results in victory over Cordelia. The final scene is crowded with incidents. Lear and Cordelia are sent to prison, followed by Edmund's executioner, Regan and Goneril quarrel publicly over Edmund, and Edgar arrives to challenge Edmund and fatally wounds him. This is followed by the news of Gloucester's death and the bodies of Goneril and Regan. Lear enters with the body of Cordelia so that the sisters are reunited in death. The revealing of the disguised Kent shows Lear's mind to be turning again and he dies.

Activity 6

a) Go through the text and find all the hints about time passing that you can. Work out how long the action of the play takes in terms of the events in the play.

b) Discuss whether the audience would be conscious of this timing during a performance (which would normally take two to three hours).

Setting

The action of *King Lear* takes place in ancient pre-Christian Britain. The play moves quickly from place to place, from inside to outside, and vice versa. The first scene in Lear's palace is the only time this location is used and the rest of Act 1 moves between Gloucester's castle and Albany's palace. Acts 2 and 3 take place in and around Gloucester's castle, which seems to stand on a windswept heath but is also strangely accessible. Act 5 starts on the heath but then moves to Dover with a couple of brief interludes at Albany's palace and Gloucester's castle. The whole of Act 5 is set in the warring camps at Dover.

The idea of place – of geography and location – is notoriously vague in *King Lear*. When Lear divides his kingdom, the language is deliberately vague: 'from this line to this' and 'this ample third of our fair kingdom' (*Act 1, Scene 1*). There is no indication of where Lear's castle is situated and, although we know that Gloucester, Albany and Cornwall live within a few hours' ride of each other, we only know that they are not too far from Dover. In a performance of the play, this is not noticeable and the locations are related more to an interior geography than to a sense of place. The heath, in its primitive wildness, is the place where human beings test their powers of survival and it is set against the solidity and comfort of Gloucester's castle.

In an interesting inversion, it is in the 'safety' of the castle – the construction that stands for civilization – where the worst cruelty and betrayal happens. Goneril and Regan strip Lear of everything and shut him out of the castle, and Edmund betrays Gloucester to Cornwall, which ends in his blinding. Meanwhile the barren heath brings out the kindness and compassion inside those who suffer its harsh environment. Kent cares for the king and Lear himself shows care for the Fool: 'I have one part in my heart / That's sorry yet for thee' (*Act 3, Scene 2*).

Writing about plot and structure

In order to gain high marks in an exam question you will need to have a thorough knowledge and understanding of the plot and structure of the play. If you are asked to evaluate a theme within the text, or the role of a character in the actions and outcomes of the play, or the dramatic significance of a section of text, a clear understanding of the sequence of events, the plot devices and the overall structure of the play is necessary.

Biography of William Shakespeare

- William Shakespeare was born in 1564 to John and Mary Shakespeare in Stratford-upon-Avon.

- He was the eldest of four boys. His parents also had four girls, three of whom died in childhood. The child mortality rate meant that Lear's curse on Goneril in Act 1, Scene 4 would have been even more shocking to Shakespeare's audience than to us.

- William's father was a glover and grain merchant, who became a town councillor. His mother Mary Arden inherited lands from her father's farm.

- From the age of seven, William is thought to have attended the local King Edward VI Grammar School, where he would have had a good grounding in Latin, grammar and rhetoric, which he used so effectively in his plays. He would also have studied Greek and Roman dramatists and poets.

Shakespeare's *King Lear* was first performed on Boxing Day in 1606

- At the age of 18, Shakespeare became involved with an older woman, Anne Hathaway, which resulted in a marriage when she was seven months pregnant. Their daughter Susanna was followed later by twins Judith and Hamnet in 1585, after which Shakespeare disappears from the records for several years.

- By 1592, he was sufficiently established in London's theatrical world to provoke a jealous review from the rival playwright Robert Greene, who wrote:

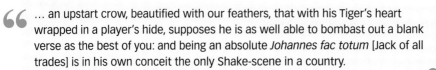

> … an upstart crow, beautified with our feathers, that with his Tiger's heart wrapped in a player's hide, supposes he is as well able to bombast out a blank verse as the best of you: and being an absolute *Johannes fac totum* [Jack of all trades] is in his own conceit the only Shake-scene in a country.
>
> (Robert Greene, *Greene's Groatsworth of Wit Bought with a Million of Repentance*, 1592)

- By 1594, Shakespeare was a partner in The Lord Chamberlain's Men along with Richard Burbage the actor and Will Kempe the comedian. It became the most successful stage company in London. He also had a share in the Globe Theatre and was the first playwright to sell written copies of his plays in mid-career. His company was a favourite with Queen Elizabeth I, who summoned them to perform for her each Christmas.

- In 1598, Shakespeare bought New Place, the second largest house in Stratford, and in due course he purchased more land and property, so he was clearly successful both in the theatre and in his other business enterprises.

- When King James I ascended the throne, Shakespeare's company found favour with a monarch who loved drama and they became The King's Men. Shakespeare may well have continued to travel between Stratford and London up to the time of his early death in 1616 at the age of 52. The cause of his death is not recorded but, some years later, the local vicar recorded in his notebook, 'Shakespeare, Drayton and Ben Jonson had a merry meeting and, it seems, drank too hard, for Shakespeare died of a fever there contracted'. His friends Heminges and Condell produced the First Folio of his plays and sonnets in 1623.

- Shakespeare is buried in the chancel of Holy Trinity Church in Stratford-upon-Avon, to which he had paid a most generous tithe. There is a bust of him set in the wall and he is said to have composed his own epitaph, which reads:

Good friend, for Jesus' sake forbear,
To dig the dust enclosed here.
Blest be the man that spares these stones,
And cursed be he that moves my bones.

(William Shakespeare, *Epitaph*, 1616)

Political background

When *King Lear* was written, around 1606, King James VI of Scotland had succeeded to the English throne as James I, after Elizabeth I had died without an heir. This meant that, for the first time, England, Scotland and Wales were joined under the crown, although they were not yet a single entity as Great Britain. James was the first Stuart king of England and he was naturally concerned that his new kingdom should be united. This is one of the main themes that Shakespeare includes in his play.

James was also a firm believer in absolute monarchy and the divine right of kings. Symbolized by the anointing at the coronation, this doctrine stated that kings held their power directly from God. As James phrased it to parliament:

Kings are justly called Gods for that they exercise a manner or resemblance of divine power upon earth. For if you will consider the attributes of God, you shall see how they agree in the person of a King. God has the power to create and destroy; make or unmake at his pleasure; to give life or send death; to judge all and to be judged, nor accountability to none; to raise low things and to make high things low at his pleasure. And the like power have Kings.

(King James I, *Works*, 1609)

This viewpoint, carried on by James's son, Charles I, later led to the English Civil War (1642–1651). For Shakespeare and his contemporaries, however, the monarch was regarded as the head of the nation, with the people as its body. Any disturbances or problems with the monarch had a profound effect on the whole country.

This is another theme Shakespeare explores in *King Lear*. Kings were set above mere mortals; as a gentleman says of the mad Lear, '**A sight most pitiful in the meanest wretch, / Past speaking of in a king!**' (*Act 4, Scene 6*).

James took his responsibilities as monarch seriously and wrote a guide to kingship for his sons. He also wrote his famous *Daemonologie* book on witchcraft, and was proud of his poetry. Possibly his greatest achievement was the beautiful translation of the Bible that he commissioned, now known as the King James Bible. His own authorship may have led him to an appreciation of Shakespeare's and to his granting of his royal charter to The King's Men. There is no record of his reaction to *King Lear* but, given his views on monarchy, he can hardly have approved of Lear's ill-judged division of his kingdom or his abdication of responsibility for his country.

Activity 1

The idea of absolute monarchy and the divine right of kings is present throughout *King Lear*.

a) Find at least one reference in each of the five acts that shows this whether through its presence or absence.

b) Find at least one reference in each act that shows what happens when this precept is ignored.

Social background

One of the principal beliefs in Europe at this time was that there was a predestined hierarchy – the Great Chain of Being. This hierarchy of order had God at the top, with angels below him, humans below angels, then animals, vegetables and inanimate matter. There were also hierarchies within each level of existence – orders of angels, of humans, of animals and so on. In addition, there were 'correspondences' between them, so that the four elements comprising the Earth corresponded with the four humours making up a person's body. A human being was seen as a microcosm of the universe. There were even hierarchies within the mental faculties, so that reason was the highest (nearest to the angels) and instincts the lowest (nearest to the beasts).

It was thought that when all these various orders were in balance – reason ruling the senses, the king ruling his subjects and fathers ruling their children – then there was harmony. However, if they became disordered, then this had an impact on the corresponding orders. When Lear no longer rules, the families and the kingdom split apart, the elements themselves turn destructive, and chaos and madness result.

Shakespeare's England was a country where everyone knew their place and what was expected of them, even down to the clothes they were allowed to wear. The Tudors had encouraged the aspirations of a rising middle class, like Shakespeare's own family, by establishing grammar schools where boys could be educated to become civil servants, lawyers, clerks, merchants, clergy and physicians.

Drawing of the Great Chain of Being, published in *Rhetorica Christiana*, by Diego de Valadés, in 1579

The unskilled labourers were the worst off in this society. The flourishing cloth-making industry had caused much agricultural land to be turned over to sheep grazing and many country labourers lost their jobs. There was little call for unskilled labour in the growing towns, so they were often reduced to severe poverty. The plight of the old, the infirm and the outcasts of society is one that is movingly portrayed by Shakespeare in *King Lear*. The Elizabethan poor laws divided them into 'deserving' and 'undeserving' poor. The first category included the elderly, the sick and children, while the second category included those who were able to work but didn't. The deserving poor were given food, clothing and shelter, while the undeserving poor were punished for begging.

As Poor Tom, Edgar was not only a beggar but a vagrant. Since Elizabethan charity was given by a person's parish, vagrancy was punished by whipping before the person was returned to their home parish. It is quite likely that Shakespeare would have seen the 'Bedlam beggars' as Edgar's description is so detailed. The way that Shakespeare presents Poor Tom's treatment by Lear, Kent and Gloucester suggests that people were not especially unkind to those suffering with mental illness. Most such sufferers were living amongst their families and the local community would have known them.

The position of women in Shakespeare's England was generally one of subservience. Even Elizabeth I felt the need to claim that her power as a monarch was despite her gender. In her famous Tilbury address she announced, 'Although I have the body of a weak and feeble woman, I have the heart and stomach of a king.' This implies that women were generally regarded as in need of guidance and protection by men. Upper-class women had more freedom in England than those in the lower classes, but most females had very little schooling except in religious observation, which taught them to obey their husbands, fathers and brothers. One of the reasons that Goneril and Regan would have been viewed as evil by Shakespeare's audience is their lack of respect for Lear and, in Goneril's case, for Albany.

Marriage, especially in the middle and upper classes, was a question of financial arrangement and a woman was expected to bring a dowry in exchange for the security and position offered by her husband. When Lear says his daughters' portions of the kingdom are their dowries, he is offering something of enormous value, which causes Burgundy to reject Cordelia without it. For Shakespeare's audience, the generosity of France in accepting Cordelia without a dowry would have been significant.

Both women and men were expected to marry and have children. Women often died in childbirth – neither Lear nor Gloucester's children have mothers still living – and they often had to grieve for dead children. Women worked, as well as men, whether spinning wool, milking cows or brewing ale. Upper-class women had to run large households, which would be the equivalent of a medium-sized business nowadays. Goneril is undoubtedly in charge at Albany's palace and Cordelia is responsible for the French army.

England's relationships with her neighbours across the Channel were generally neutral in Shakespeare's time, except with the Spanish, whose navy was powerful and who were bent on colonizing South America. The invasion of the Spanish Armada in August 1588 is a famous episode of history. There were generally marriages between European royal families, so there was nothing unusual about Lear choosing Burgundy and France as Cordelia's suitors. Cordelia may have brought the French army to Lear's rescue, but Shakespeare could not present them as defeating the British, as this would have been regarded as unpatriotic.

Activity 2

Design a short presentation using ideas from the Great Chain of Being to show the relationship between the following:

- Lear's abdication and the destruction of the kingdom
- Lear's injustice as a father and the fragmentation of his family
- the reflection of these breakdowns in order on the cosmos itself.

You will need to look at how each of the above events disrupts the 'natural' order of the chain.

Tips for assessment

While you are not expected to have a detailed knowledge of Elizabethan and Jacobean England, you will gain marks for commenting on aspects of context relevant to the play and the points you are making.

Religion and superstition

Religion in Shakespeare's England was an important part of everyday life. The Reformation begun by Henry VIII in 1529 had led to upheaval in society, and the brief and brutal restoration of Catholicism by Mary Tudor (1553–1558) made Elizabeth I wary of religious persecution. She generally left Catholics alone unless they stirred up trouble, and James I, though a Protestant king, was tolerant of Catholics who took the Oath of Allegiance and 'any that will be quiet and give but an outward obedience to the law'. Christianity underpinned the behaviour expected of people and church-going was compulsory at least once a month. In practice, most people attended services on Sundays and schoolchildren read the Bible every day. It was customary for children to kneel and request a blessing from their parents at the start of each day, a custom seen in *King Lear* when the king is taken to prison with Cordelia: 'When thou dost ask me blessing, I'll kneel down, / And ask of thee forgiveness' (Act 5, Scene 3).

In spite of their Christian beliefs and practices, Elizabethans were very superstitious. Alongside witches, a belief in devils and demons created superstitious stories and fears, and a whole hierarchy of demons was identified. King James's book *Daemonologie*, written and published in 1597, showed his own keen interest in the subject and Shakespeare uses many references to demons in *King Lear* (see page 30).

It is not surprising that a poorly educated population, without the benefit of modern science, should seek for explanations of misfortune. People were brought up in a religion that stressed the primacy of the soul and taught that heaven and angels were engaged in a permanent battle with hell and devils over people's souls. The stars and planets were also regarded as having special powers and astrology was treated with reverence. The Earth was seen as the centre of the universe, surrounded by stars and planets, which influenced human events. The horoscope cast at someone's birth might foretell what kind of life they would have and the various juxtapositions of the planets could forecast good or bad luck. These ideas are seen in *King Lear* as well as many other of Shakespeare's plays.

One of the main metaphorical ideas of the time was of Fortune as a blindfolded goddess with a wheel. She was blindfolded because she was impartial and everyone on her wheel was going either up or down. This meant that when you were at the bottom, you had the consolation of knowing you would have to go up, but those at the top knew they would not stay there forever. Kent's appeal when he is in the stocks, 'Fortune, good night; smile once more; turn thy wheel!' (*Act 2, Scene 2*), would have been recognized by Shakespeare's audience. Fortune was also regarded as the Fool calls her, 'Fortune, that arrant whore' (*Act 2, Scene 4*), because she bestowed her favour indiscriminately.

The Wheel of Fortune from an illuminated copy of the *Troy Book*, first printed in 1513

Activity 3

Imagine you have been asked to write a short article of 300 words for a student magazine. The title is 'Fortune and the stars in *King Lear*'. You should include:

- references to the stars and planets in the play and what Elizabethans believed
- references to Fortune in the play and how this metaphor was perceived by Shakespeare's contemporaries.

Health and sickness

The natural world contained many mysteries for the Elizabethans and their explanations tended towards magic and natural remedies. Before treating a sick patient, a physician would commonly cast the patient's horoscope to identify the right moment for giving remedies. They believed that people were subject to the four humours (choleric, phlegmatic, sanguinary and melancholic), which corresponded to organs of the body. An excess of the fluid in any of these organs could lead to sickness and even death. Goneril refers to Lear's 'infirm and choleric years' (*Act 1, Scene 1*). The humours were organized around the four elements and each was subject to a planetary influence and related to a specific season of the year. In *King Lear*, Cordelia's doctor explains, 'Our foster-nurse of nature is repose, / The which he lacks' (*Act 4, Scene 4*). He says that he has 'many simples operative, whose power / Will close the eye of anguish' (*Act 4, Scene 4*), the herbal equivalent of modern sleeping tablets.

The Elizabethans were prone to many diseases, although the most feared was the Black Death, which had wiped out a third of European citizens in the 14th century. Outbreaks continued until well into the 17th century, causing theatres and other public places to be shut for fear of spreading infection. In addition, people had to contend with typhus, smallpox, syphilis and, in London at any rate, malaria. The only remedies available were bloodletting, through cutting or the use of leeches, which was thought to bring down fever, and the use of medicinal herbs. Vinegar was the all-purpose antiseptic. Add to this the number of women who died in childbirth and the afflictions of rheumatism and gout, as well as everyday accidental deaths and injuries, and it was more surprising to find people living into old age than not.

There were some curious beliefs to try and explain certain symptoms, such as the 'wandering womb', which was said to cause convulsions, heart tremors and shortness of breath in women. When he hears from Kent about Regan and Cornwall's responsibility for setting him in the stocks, Lear exclaims, 'O how this mother swells up toward my heart! / Hysteria passio! Down, thou climbing sorrow!' (*Act 2, Scene 4*). He appears to be comparing his rising emotion with this supposed affliction in women and therefore implying that his feelings show weakness.

Activity 4

Find the following references in the text of *King Lear* and discuss what you learn from the play about contemporary medical beliefs:

- the notion of Lear as 'choleric' (above)

- the exclamation from Lear about 'this mother' (above)

- the treatment proposed by the servants for Gloucester's bleeding eyes in Act 3, Scene 7

- the cure for Lear's madness prescribed by the doctor to Cordelia in Act 4, Scene 4

- the description of the deaths of Gloucester and Lear in Act 5, Scene 3.

Theatre and entertainment

The Globe Theatre on London's Southbank is a faithful recreation of Shakespeare's theatre, even down to its methods of construction. The London around it has changed considerably though – the original Globe was next to a bear garden, where bears and bulls were baited for sport. The audience is also considerably better behaved now than in Shakespeare's time, when there were many complaints about the rowdiness of the theatre crowds. The audience would have seen a good number of plays, as the company would perform as many as ten different plays in a fortnight. Rehearsal times were very short and actors would have only their lines and cues to go on. There was no such thing as copyright, so clerks from rival companies would sit in the audience taking down as much of the play as they could manage. Some theatres were also associated with gambling and brothels, so it is not surprising that they weren't considered respectable places. Employers also accused theatres of drawing their apprentices away from work, as plays were performed in the afternoons, while it was still light.

The modern Globe Theatre with an audience rather better behaved than its counterpart in Shakespeare's day

Other entertainments varied from the lavish masques performed at court, bull- and bear-baiting and cock-fighting, to visiting fairs and markets and taking part in drinking, gambling and fighting. At these fairs and markets, couples could meet and join in the dancing. Encouraged by Elizabeth I, dancing was a popular diversion, from sophisticated court dances like the lively galliard or the stately pavane, to the country and Morris dancing of the lower classes. It was the custom in Shakespeare's time to end a play with a dance or masque and music was a big part of Elizabethan celebrations whether it was produced by a single fiddler or piper, a group of instrumentalists or a church choir.

Sports and games were also very popular and ranged from cards, dice, chess and backgammon to more energetic sports like tennis and bowls. Noblemen would go hunting, as Lear does while staying with Goneril, with a group of huntsmen and gamekeepers, and usually for deer.

Other pastimes included billiards, archery and wrestling, while children enjoyed marbles, hopscotch and Blind Man's Buff. Football had been banned in the Middle Ages because it was regarded as too rough (it was rather different from the modern game) and because it was more useful to practise archery in case men were needed for the army. In Shakespeare's time, football was played only in the streets by idle boys using a blown-up pig's bladder. Kent refers to Oswald as a 'base foot-ball player' (*Act 1, Scene 4*).

Crime and punishment

As in everything else, crimes and punishments often depended on your class and social status. The system of justice was very different from modern times and prisons were only used for remand before trial. Trial was before a judge or magistrate and there was no jury. The trial was heavily biased in favour of the prosecution and the defendant would have little hope of legal representation. Many crimes carried the death penalty, including witchcraft.

Prostitutes and beggars would be whipped. In his madness, Lear rails at the state of justice in his kingdom, pardoning an imaginary adulterer and asking, 'Why dost thou lash that whore?' (*Act 4, Scene 6*). Thieves and fraudsters would be put in the pillory or the stocks where the crowd could deal out justice of a kind by pelting them with filth. When Cornwall puts Kent in the stocks, he is treating the king's ambassador like a common felon, which is why Lear is so enraged.

In addition to the magistrates, there were ecclesiastical courts, which dealt with many misdemeanours from adultery and incest to non-attendance at church or not baptizing a child. Offenders were brought before ecclesiastical courts by summoners, who were dreaded. Lear describes the storm as 'These dreadful summoners' (*Act 3, Scene 2*).

Activity 5

Look at the following extracts and write a list of the sort of crimes that might have been condemned in Shakespeare's England:

- Act 3, Scene 2, from **'Let the great gods…'** to **'…These dreadful summoners grace.'**

- Act 4, Scene 6, from **'A man may see how this world…'** to **'…harder, harder; so.'**

Shakespeare's sources for *King Lear*

Although *King Lear* is supposedly set in pre-Roman Britain, most of the setting is Shakespeare's England. The characters are allegedly pagan and Shakespeare has them addressing Roman gods such as Apollo, Jove and Juno long before Romans arrived in Britain. Another anachronism is that the themes of moral corruption and redemption evident in the play are decidedly Christian in nature. In Shakespeare's time, it was safer to set a story that involved the downfall of a king, particularly through his own moral blindness, in a dim and distant past.

James's love of theatre meant that The King's Men were called to perform ten times a year, which meant they soon ran out of material and Shakespeare needed to write more plays. He may have been influenced by the famous Gunpowder Plot of 5 November 1605, just over a year before *King Lear* was first performed. The plot was intended to blow up the royal family and parliament. It led to the arrest of prominent men, some of whom were related to Shakespeare's family, giving him, perhaps, an added impetus to write a play that would reflect the dangerous and uncertain times that people were living through. It is not hard to see parallels in *King Lear* with the destruction of a royal family and a whole kingdom.

One of Shakespeare's sources was an anonymous play, *The True Chronicle History of King Leir*, published in 1605, but probably performed before then. The main plot of this play also features the king dividing his kingdom between his three daughters, but creates a happy ending with Lear and Cordelia ruling a kingdom once more in harmony. This earlier play, like Shakespeare's, was probably based on the same story in Holinshed's *Chronicles of England, Scotland and Ireland*, published in 1587. Holinshed, in turn, would have known the tale from Geoffrey of Monmouth's *Historia Regium Britanniae*, a history of Britain written in the 12th century. The ending of the 1605 play was based on this account, although it omits the final part when Cordelia is deposed by her sisters' sons and hangs herself.

This ending can be found in two other sources that Shakespeare may have used – *The Mirror for Magistrates*, a collection of poems published in 1574 that recounts the fall of great men and some stanzas from Edmund Spenser's epic verse drama 'The Faerie Queene', published in 1590, which also tell the story of Lear. In the same year, Philip Sidney published *The Countess of Pembroke's Arcadia* in which the tale of a father and two sons appears. This seems to have been the source from which Shakespeare drew the Gloucester subplot, which mirrors and enriches the main plot of *King Lear*.

Shakespeare's play also reflects James I's own fascination with demonic possession. Much of the dialogue given to the mad Lear and to Edgar as Poor Tom reflects on ideas in Samuel Harsnett's *A Declaration of Egregious Popish Impostures*, 1603, a treatise against Catholic exorcisms and the casting out of devils that gives details of methods and types of possession. Many of the names of the demons addressed by Poor Tom are taken from this work, as when he refers to Gloucester as 'the foul Flibbertigibbet' (*Act 3, Scene 4*).

Shakespeare also gives Poor Tom some lines that muddle up an ancient and lost Scottish ballad with the fairy tale 'Jack and the Beanstalk':

Child Rowland to the dark tower came,
His word was still: Fie, foh, and fum,
I smell the blood of a British man.
(Edgar, Act 3, Scene 4)

Child Rowland ('Child' meant apprentice knight) was the subject of many ballads and stories, and the first line above was later used by Robert Browning as the title of a poem written in 1855.

Shakespeare uses other snatches of old songs to give Edgar's Poor Tom credibility in Act 3, Scene 6. Lear, his own wits turned, has decided that Poor Tom is a classical philosopher, referring to him in Act 3, Scene 4 as 'learned Theban' and 'good Athenian', which recalls the Ancient Greek philosophers.

 Activity 6

Look up the sources from which Shakespeare drew his story and write three sentences for each, showing how each source differs from Shakespeare's version of *King Lear*.

Writing about context

Although you will not be questioned directly on the context of *King Lear*, to gain the higher grades you will be expected to relate events or themes in the play to the time and society in which the play was written. Shakespeare's world was very different to our own, but the humans who lived in it were much the same. If you can distinguish between the universal ideas and behaviour shown by Shakespeare, and those particular to his time, the examiner will note it.

Drama

Drama is normally presented through the medium of performance. The story is told through dialogue and action rather than narrative. Poetry and novels may be read aloud, and even dramatized, but are more often experienced by an individual reading the words on the page. However, when you study a play, always remember that it was intended for performance, so it is important to read it aloud with others and to watch it as a production. Watching or participating in a performance will affect your understanding of the text. The director and actors for each production will perform their own interpretation of the play. A good production will illuminate the writer's intentions and make the audience think carefully about the play's meaning.

Drama originated in Ancient Greece, where it derived its two main forms of comedy and tragedy. A comedy is a play that is not necessarily funny but ends happily; a tragedy is a play that ends sadly, usually with the death of the **protagonist**.

King Lear is a tragedy, which means it is a serious play involving the downfall and death of the protagonist. Well-known Ancient Greek playwrights of tragedy, like Aeschylus, Euripides and Sophocles, created a tradition that the Greek philosopher Aristotle defined in his book, *Poetics* in the 4th century BCE. He suggested that tragedy must be about an important subject; that tragic protagonists must have greatness, or magnitude, that marks them out as special; that tragedy must use rhythm, harmony and song in its language; and it must be performed rather than read, so that the audience will feel pity and fear for the character(s), leading to catharsis of these emotions, so that they leave the theatre feeling renewed.

> **catharsis** purging of emotions created by the play, so that the audience feel restored
>
> **protagonist** the main character or tragic hero

Activity 1

Read the story of King Lear in a book such as *Lamb's Tales from Shakespeare* by Charles and Mary Lamb, 1807 (an online version is also available). Discuss the differences between reading the tale as a story to yourself and seeing it performed on a stage or even as a film. Why do you think Aristotle considered tragedy should be performed?

Does *King Lear* conform to Aristotle's ideas of tragedy?

The play concerns the downfall of the most important person in the country – the head of state – and his descent into poverty and madness, so it fulfils the idea of magnitude. At the start of the play Lear is shown as a monarch in control of his kingdom, at the centre of his court, surrounded by nobles and retainers sworn to obey him. Even his family feel bound to do his bidding, as Shakespeare makes clear when Goneril and Regan try to outperform each other in hypocritical protestations of love. Those who stand against him – Cordelia and Kent – are dealt with promptly and ruthlessly, despite being his favourite daughter and his most loyal courtier. Lear tells the king of France, 'we / Have no such daughter', and banishes Kent, threatening that if he is found 'in our dominions, / The moment is thy death' *(Act 1, Scene 1)*. These are the same dominions he is about to divide between Goneril and Regan.

From Lear's decisions in this scene, the audience witnesses an inevitable progress towards his loss of power, without which he can no longer command. From this stems his loss of authority over his daughters and their husbands, which, lacking the filial affection they so loudly declared, leads in turn to his loss of followers, of shelter and even of reason. Finally, it leads to the destruction of his family, his kingdom and his life. He could not have held a higher position nor suffered a more complete fall.

Activity 2

Find evidence, in the form of references and/or quotations, to support each of the statements listed below. Draw up a grid, like the one below, and complete it with your answers.

Statement	Reference	Quotation
At the start of the play King Lear is in command of his kingdom and his court.		
The courtiers defer to him and obey his wishes.		
His two elder daughters respect his commands.		
Lear cannot believe Cordelia will defy him.		
Lear cannot believe Kent would speak against him.		

King Lear is written to be performed on a stage and the story is told through actors and dialogue, so it fulfils Aristotle's criteria for performance. Greek drama took place in an amphitheatre built in a circle around the stage, which gave it natural acoustics. Shakespeare's tragedies took place in theatres like The Globe, but no doubt the Ancient Greek and Elizabethan audiences would have had similar human emotions in response to the dramas, in spite of their different cultural backgrounds.

Drama in Shakespeare's theatre followed a tradition of medieval miracle and morality plays, which were associated with the Catholic religion and sought to educate the population about the Bible and the way they should live. Audiences were therefore used to theatre that had a moral purpose, generally showing the good being rewarded and the wicked punished.

Some of Shakespeare's finest language can be found in this play, including metre in the form of **blank verse**, harmony in its use of poetic and figurative language, and song in both literal form and the rhythms of some of the speeches. (See the Language chapter for further discussion.)

Aristotle also suggested that the tragic protagonist's fall is caused by **hamartia**, which by Shakespeare's time was seen as a fatal flaw in the protagonist's character that causes their downfall. Lear's error seems to be what Aristotle defines as the most frequent hamartia – **hubris** – as well as a dangerous inability to distinguish between honesty and flattery. Although the game of 'who loves me most' may well be proposed in a friendly spirit, it quickly degenerates when Cordelia refuses to play: 'How, how, Cordelia! Mend your speech a little, / Lest you may mar your fortunes' *(Act 1, Scene 1)*. The blindness that causes Lear to believe the words of Goneril and Regan is already evident in his belief that he can give away his kingdom – and thus his power – and still be treated as king. These flaws lead to **nemesis**, which is amply demonstrated in Lear's downfall.

The relationship of suffering to right or wrong actions is central to tragedy. In *King Lear*, as in the Greek tragedy of *Oedipus Rex*, the retribution seems out of proportion to the offence. For Aristotle, tragedy also depends on the audience being able to see existing or potentially admirable qualities in the protagonist. However, in the opening scene, a modern audience will find little to like or admire in King Lear. It is only as he begins to feel the force of the nemesis he has unleashed that we can see his potential as a man and the monarch he might have been.

Lear, played by Antony Sher, is enthroned as a king used to his own power, showing little to admire as he pronounces judgement over Cordelia in the Royal Shakespeare Company production in 2016

The other element identified by Aristotle is **peripeteia**, the turning point or reversal of fortune that usually occurs around the third act or climax of a classical play. In *King Lear*, many people see this as the moment when Lear is shut out of Gloucester's castle and forced into the storm without food or shelter. Others may see it even earlier when Goneril tells Lear to dismiss some of his followers.

> **blank verse** unrhymed verse; the five beats in each line are known as **iambic pentameter**
>
> **hamartia** a mistake made by the protagonist, which leads to their downfall
>
> **hubris** excessive or stubborn pride
>
> **iambic pentameter** a rhythm, a line of five sets of syllables, each set with the stress on the second syllable, e.g. 'To **shake** all **cares** and **bus**iness **from** our **age**'
>
> **nemesis** divine retribution
>
> **peripeteia** the point at which things change for the protagonist and the audience can see his fortunes are in decline

Activity 3

Discuss the peripeteia in *King Lear*. Write a paragraph giving your view of when it occurs, supported by evidence from the play.

Is King Lear a tragic hero?

This is the question that leads to conflict about the play's genre. In Aristotelian tragedy, the great man is brought low by hamartia and by fate. The tragedy lies in seeing someone noble with great potential being deprived of their position, their belongings and all they love. The courage with which the protagonist fights against nemesis, although they cannot win, is the standard by which they are judged. In Shakespeare's *King Lear*, however, although Lear bravely defies the storm – 'Blow, winds, and crack your cheeks! rage! blow!' *(Act 3, Scene 2)* – he is judged as a human being rather than as a great king.

The famous critic, A.C. Bradley said the play should be called 'The Redemption of King Lear' (*Shakespearean Tragedy*, 1904) and this is one interpretation that suggests a departure from Aristotelian tragedy. There are many references to Fortune and her wheel, ideas taken from medieval drama, although also based on the idea of fate taking a hand in human affairs. For those who see *King Lear* as a Christian drama, it is the struggle between good and evil that is at the play's core rather than the idea of a noble person contending against the gods.

There should also be some traits worthy of admiration in a tragic hero, but few members of an audience will be drawn to King Lear at the play's opening. The critic Jan Kott says, 'Regarded as a person, a character, Lear is ridiculous, naive and stupid. When he goes mad, he can only arouse compassion, never pity and terror.' (*Shakespeare Our Contemporary*, 1963) However, A.C. Bradley maintains that 'a long life of absolute power, in which he has been flattered to the top of his bent, has produced in him that blindness to human limitations, and that presumptuous self-will, which in Greek tragedy we have so often seen stumbling against the altar of Nemesis' (*Shakespearean Tragedy,* 1904).

Audiences are more likely to sympathize with Lear as a human being after he has been cast out with nothing and left to suffer in the storm; here Anthony Hopkins plays Lear in the National Theatre production in 2002

Activity 4

In the first scene of the play, Lear is shown sowing the seeds of his own downfall. Discuss which of the following character traits you consider important in contributing to this process:

- pride
- vanity
- self-will
- moral blindness
- love for his children
- old age.

Write one sentence for each trait you select, explaining how you think it contributed to Lear's downfall.

The problem with the ending

One of the most frequently asked questions about Shakespeare's play is 'Why does Cordelia die?' For many years *King Lear* was performed with a happy ending (see the Performance chapter) but that runs counter to its writing as a tragedy. For A.C. Bradley it demonstrates 'the contrast between the outward and the inward, Cordelia's death and Cordelia's soul' (*Shakespearean Tragedy*, 1904). He argues that her death is less important than 'what she is'. Kenneth Muir, in his introduction to the Arden edition of *King Lear* (1966), argues that the fact of her death, pointless though it may seem, is secondary to its effect on Lear: 'It destroys his dream of a happy life in prison, and it hastens his final dissolution…'.

The manner of Lear's death is ambiguous. Lear's final words are: 'Do you see this? Look on her, look, her lips, / Look there, look there!' *(Act 5, Scene 3)*. Bradley suggests that Lear dies of joy, believing Cordelia to be alive. Others find no such meaning, implying that Lear's words mean only that Cordelia's ability to speak is reduced to 'nothing' – her first word to Lear in the play. The wish to find some catharsis, some hopeful sign in the ending, is understandable but more likely to be disappointed. The triumph of good, such as it is, is reduced to Edgar, who seems to find little comfort in the prospect of ruling the kingdom: 'we that are young / Shall never see so much, nor live so long' *(Act 5, Scene 3)*. The bleakness of the ending reflects the endless suffering that permeates the play itself. According to the critic Harold Bloom, the Lear universe lacks hope and so does the ending:

 'Lear is the universal image of the unwisdom and destructiveness of paternal love at its most ineffectual, implacably persuaded of its own benignity, totally devoid of self-knowledge, and careering onward until it brings down the person it loves best, and its world as well.'

(Harold Bloom, *Shakespeare - The Invention of the Human*, 1998)

Another critic, J. Stampfer, believes that the tragic ending is integral to the cathartic effect experienced by the audience:

 [the audience] 'shares and releases the most private and constricting fear to which mankind is subject, the fear that penance is impossible… that we inhabit an imbecile universe. It is by this vision of reality that Lear lays down his life for his folly. Within its bounds lies the catharsis of Shakespeare's profoundest tragedy.'

(J. Stampfer, 'The Catharsis of King Lear', 1960)

Tips for assessment

You do not need to reach a conclusion about the ending of the play. It is more important to show that you have an understanding of the interpretations that have been put on it and that Shakespeare has, perhaps deliberately, left it ambiguous so that audiences can decide for themselves.

Activity 5

a) Discuss the various viewpoints about the ending of *King Lear*. What would be the effect of each of the following options?

- Lear rescues Cordelia from being hanged and is restored to his throne.

- Lear speaks his last words, imagining Cordelia is alive.

- Lear dies knowing Cordelia is dead and her mouth is closed forever.

b) If you were directing a performance of the play, which interpretation would you want from the actor playing Lear, and why?

Shakespearean tragedy

The critic David Chandler writes:

> 'The essence of Shakespeare's tragedies is the expression of one of the great paradoxes of life. We might call it the paradox of disappointment. Defeat, shattered hopes, and ultimately death face us all as human beings. They are very real, but somehow we have the intuitive feeling that they are out of place. They seem to be intruders into life. Tragic literature confronts us afresh with this paradox and we become fascinated by it.'
>
> (David Chandler, 'The Essence of Shakespearean Tragedy', 1960)

He continues by arguing that each of Shakespeare's main tragedies is about a single man. These characters are portrayed vividly as real human beings, which enables the audience to identify with them. Each play contains a hope that is disappointed or an ambition that is frustrated. Each play ends with the death of the protagonist and the defeat of their hopes and/or ambitions. This leaves the audience with a paradox – that the ending does not assert that life is meaningful in spite of this nor that our hopes are worthless and we should despair. Instead, we are invited to consider the situation and find our own meaning.

Shakespeare's tragedies usually have a protagonist who is noble but has a character flaw that leads to their undoing. There are usually external influences that affect the character's behaviour and destiny. In *King Lear*, these influences are Lear's daughters, but also the forces of fate, or Fortune. The play opens with order and harmony and then descends into chaos and disunity, ending in death.

Unlike Aristotelian tragedy, Shakespeare's tragedies do not observe the three unities. Aristotle wrote that a tragedy should take place in a single location on a single day and should have a single subject. *King Lear* ranges over a number of locations from Lear's palace, via the heath round Gloucester's castle, to Dover, where the final action happens. It also takes place over several weeks and it has a subplot concerning Gloucester and his two sons.

The conflict at the heart of Shakespeare's tragedies is often symbolized by storms or madness, which show the internal conflict of the protagonist as well as the onset of chaos. Usually, they end in violence, maybe with a battle or a duel of some kind, as well as the inevitable death of the tragic hero. While the military battle in *King Lear* is won by the forces of evil, the duel between Edgar and Edmund is won by the force for good, and order is therefore established.

Elements of comedy

Greek tragedies did not have any comedy in them. Greek playwrights kept the two genres strictly apart. However, Shakespeare uses comedy in his tragic dramas in order to make them more realistic. He also uses it to enhance the tragedy and make it seem more grievous by contrast. The Fool in *King Lear* has the job of a licensed court entertainer, but the jokes he makes at Lear's expense tell home truths. When Lear asks him if he is calling him a fool, he replies, 'All thy other titles thou hast given away; that thou wast born with' *(Act 1, Scene 4)*.

G. Wilson Knight, in his famous critique of the play, *The Wheel of Fire* (1930), says, 'The peculiar dualism at the root of this play which wrenches and splits the mind by a sight of incongruities displays in turn realities absurd, hideous, pitiful. This incongruity is Lear's madness: it is also the demonic laughter that echoes in the Lear universe.' Wilson Knight refers to this as 'the comedy of the grotesque'.

Activity 6

Find three or four examples of humour in *King Lear* and, for each of them, write a short paragraph describing how they can be seen as humorous and the effect they create on the audience.

Writing about genre

You may be asked to write about *King Lear* as a tragedy in the exam, or you may have a question related to theme or character. In any case, the genre of the play will be relevant and you should demonstrate a knowledge of how it works as tragedy and how Lear may be seen as a tragic hero. Being able to discuss and evaluate the elements of tragedy that Shakespeare uses is crucial to gaining a good grade. Remember to use the correct literary terminology when referring to tragic aspects of the play.

King Lear

As the eponymous tragic hero who gives his name to the play, Lear is at the centre of it, so it is surprising that he disappears from the action for much of the time after Act 3. His role as the tragic hero is discussed in the Genre chapter, but his dual role as king and father is essential to the play.

There is a paradox in the character of Lear. As a monarch, he has the power to reward or punish as he sees fit. People obey him because of his position not because of his character, a truth he comes to see later in the play: **'A dog's obey'd in office'** (*Act 4, Scene 6*). Yet he imagines, at the start of the drama, that he can give away his kingdom (and thus the status from which he derives his authority) and still receive the respect and obedience due to a head of state:

> **Key quotation**
>
> Only we shall retain
> The name and all th'addition to a king
> (*Lear, Act 1, Scene 1*)

At the same time, as the father of three daughters, he expects love and respect from his children, without realizing that this needs to be reciprocated. The absurd charade in which he demands that his daughters compete with each other in front of the court to show who loves him best reveals his vanity and his moral blindness. In thinking that words, rather than deeds, can prove real affection, Shakespeare presents him as lacking in judgement. As Kent points out, **'Nor are those empty-hearted whose low sounds / Reverb no hollowness'** (*Act 1, Scene 1*). His children know him better than he knows them, for Regan comments, **'he hath ever but slenderly known himself'** and Goneril says, **'The best and soundest of his time hath been but rash'** (*Act 1, Scene 1*).

As the protagonist, Lear goes on a physical journey from his own palace, via Albany's to Gloucester's castles, to Dover. He is also forced on a personal and spiritual journey, which takes him into humiliation, poverty, madness and, ultimately, redemption and death. The main paradox in his character is that, when sane and in power, he behaves foolishly and tyrannically; when he loses everything, including his sanity, he finds humility, compassion and truth.

Lear must have some good traits at the beginning of the play, since he inspires devotion in Kent and Gloucester, and love in Cordelia and the Fool. Even before his first entrance, the audience hears of his decision to divide his kingdom – a decision that seems unwise to a modern audience and far more so to an Elizabethan one. The reasons Lear gives – **'To shake all cares and business from our age'** and **'that future strife / May be prevented now'** (*Act 1, Scene 1*) – does not conceal the likely outcome of this folly.

Lear makes no secret of the fact that he loves Cordelia best and has planned to give her the largest portion and then live with her, for he tells Kent, **'I lov'd her most, and thought to set my rest / On her kind nursery'** (*Act 1, Scene 1*). When he challenges his daughters – 'Which of you shall we say doth love us most?' (*Act 1, Scene 1*), Goneril and Regan make smooth and hyperbolic protestations of their love, while Cordelia is unable to join in. Deprived of his dearest wish, Lear turns on his youngest daughter with curses out of all proportion to her 'offence' and banishes her, telling Cornwall and Albany to divide her share between them. The accusation of 'hideous rashness' made by Kent seems to be almost an understatement of his behaviour, especially when he banishes his most loyal follower for telling him, 'thou dost evil' (*Act 1, Scene 1*).

As the results of his actions become clear, Lear finds himself in conflict with his eldest daughter, who complains, 'His knights grow riotous, and himself upbraids us / On every trifle' (*Act 1, Scene 3*). However, when Goneril tells her father he must cut the number of his followers, his reaction is horrifying. Displaying the same impulsive anger he showed towards Cordelia, he curses Goneril, 'Into her womb convey sterility!' (*Act 1, Scene 4*). A few minutes later, he is in tears, announcing his departure to Regan's house, convinced she will treat him better. Not until it becomes obvious that both his daughters are united does he realize what he has done. His speech beginning, 'O! reason not the need!' is an attempt to explain that people need more 'than nature needs' but it ends with Lear raging impotently, 'I will have such revenges on you both / That all the world shall – I will do such things, / What they are, yet I know not, but they shall be / The terrors of the earth' (*Act 2, Scene 4*). As his lack of power dawns on him, he tells the Fool, 'O Fool! I shall go mad' (*Act 2, Scene 4*).

Shut out of Gloucester's castle on the wild heath, Lear faces the full force of a storm that reflects the turmoil in his mind and in his kingdom. The reversal of his fortunes is sudden and complete. His knights seem to have abandoned him, apart from one gentleman and the disguised Kent. His two older daughters have shown what their protestations of love were worth and only the Fool goes with him. As he hurls defiance at the heavens, we may begin to feel pity for him as 'A poor, infirm, weak, and despis'd old man' (*Act 3, Scene 2*). The mental instability that has been present from the start, and which he fears, grows on him as the weather takes its toll on his body.

At the heart of *King Lear* is what we could call an identity crisis. When Lear is no longer ruling as monarch and people stop obeying him, he doesn't know who he is: 'Who is it that can tell me who I am?' The Fool replies, 'Lear's shadow' (*Act 1, Scene 4*), much as we would say someone is a shadow of their former self. As Lear's grip on reason loosens, he sees the world from the perspective of 'Poor naked wretches, whereso'er you are, / That bide the pelting of this pitiless storm' (*Act 3, Scene 4*), realizing that he should have taken care of them when he was able. Now he is one of them and his mind is obsessed with his 'pelican daughters' to the point where he is convinced that only Poor Tom's 'unkind daughters' could have brought Poor Tom so low (*Act 3, Scene 4*). He identifies himself with the mad beggar to the extent that he tears off his own clothes. By the time he is arranging the mock trial of Goneril and Regan, the transformation from autocratic king to mad beggar seems complete.

After Gloucester warns Kent to take Lear to Dover, the audience doesn't see Lear again until Act 4, Scene 6, when he enters *'fantastically dressed with wild flowers'* and raving about lechery. In his madness, he sees more clearly how justice works for the rich and powerful against the poor and weak, and realizes that authority is only on the surface:

> **Key quotation**
>
> Thorough tatter'd clothes small vices do appear;
> Robes and furr'd gowns hide all
> *(Lear, Act 4, Scene 6)*

The audience has heard that Lear is too ashamed to meet Cordelia and, in the scene where they are reconciled, his waking thought is 'You do me wrong to take me out o'th'grave' (*Act 4, Scene 7*). His dream of living with Cordelia in prison where 'We two alone will sing like birds i'th'cage' (*Act 5, Scene 3*) is another delusion, horribly shattered by her tragic and unnecessary death. His cry of 'Why should a dog, a horse, a rat, have life / And thou no breath at all?' (*Act 5, Scene 3*) reveals the grief that will be understood by all those who have lost a loved one too soon.

What makes the ending so unbearable is that Lear and Cordelia never have the opportunity to spend time together, as Lear hoped at the start of the play, and his realization that all life is reduced to 'nothing' causes his hopeless repetition of 'Never, never, never, never, never!' before his heart breaks. (*Act 5, Scene 3*).

Activity 1

a) Read the two quotations below, then discuss what they tell you about how Shakespeare presents Lear's personal journey within the play.

Here I disclaim all my paternal care,
Propinquity and property of blood,
And as a stranger to my heart and me
Hold thee from this forever.
(Lear, Act 1, Scene 1)

Come let's away to prison;
We two alone will sing like birds i'th'cage:
When thou dost ask me blessing, I'll kneel down,
And ask of thee forgiveness:
(Lear, Act 5, Scene 3)

b) Create a timeline, showing the stages of Lear's journey – physical and personal – from the start of the play to the end.

Tips for assessment

You may be asked a question relating to Lear himself, or to the other characters, so be prepared to evaluate their relationships, their personalities and their role in the plot backing up your ideas with close reference to the text and quotations.

Earl of Gloucester

Gloucester opens the play in mid-conversation with Kent and it is from him that the audience first learns of Lear's plans to divide his kingdom. He also talks about Edmund, his illegitimate son, joking, 'there was good sport at his making' (*Act 1, Scene 2*), which suggests that he takes adultery lightly. He appears to know his sons as little as Lear knows his daughters for he is readily taken in by Edmund's lies about Edgar.

Like Lear, he is rash and hasty to anger, wanting Cornwall to outlaw Edgar before he has even spoken to him about the supposed plot against his life. Gloucester is, as Edmund calls him, 'a credulous father' (*Act 1, Scene 2*), something he reveals in his superstitious belief that 'These late eclipses in the sun and moon portend no good to us' (*Act 1, Scene 2*). In his blindness to his sons' real qualities, Gloucester mirrors Lear and it is not until he is physically blinded that he sees clearly which son loves him.

Gloucester remains loyal to Lear, in spite of being overridden by Cornwall and Regan in his own house. He follows Lear out onto the heath and manages to persuade him to shelter in a farmhouse where a fire and food are ready. He also warns Kent, 'I have o'erheard a plot of death upon him' and tells him to take Lear to Dover (*Act 3, Scene 6*). He returns to his castle only to be arrested and tortured by Cornwall and Regan. His downfall parallels that of Lear. From being a powerful nobleman with a castle and household, he becomes a blind beggar, wandering the countryside, dependent on the charity of his own servants and of his good son, Edgar.

He is still credulous, although perhaps with more reason because of his blindness. Determined on suicide, he believes Edgar when he tells him first that he is at the top of a high cliff and then that he has survived the fall to which he was apparently driven by a monstrous fiend. He tells Edgar that the 'miracle' has taught him to 'bear / Affliction till it do cry out itself / 'Enough, enough,' and die' (*Act 4, Scene 6*).

When Lear and Gloucester meet at Dover, the sight of the two old men – one blind and one mad – strikes the audience with pity and sadness. Gloucester knows the king by his voice and Lear eventually recognizes the earl.

Gloucester dies offstage, his death reported by Edgar, who finally revealed himself to his father. But the story of his wrongs and his suffering was too much for his father whose 'flaw'd heart… Burst smilingly' (*Act 5, Scene 3*). His death both foretells and contrasts with Lear's.

Activity 2

Create a comparison table for Lear and Gloucester, showing their similarities and differences. Include references and quotations to support your ideas.

	Similarities	Differences
Family relationships		
Personalities		
Sufferings		
Personal journeys		
Deaths		

Edmund

Edmund is a Shakespearean villain who enjoys the role. He is a **machiavellian** character, who takes the audience into his confidence in a series of soliloquies that reveal his ruthless plans to obtain and keep power. He does it with an enjoyment at his own cleverness, **'Now, gods, stand up for bastards!'** (*Act 1, Scene 2*). His comments about his father show some justification as he reflects on his father's superstitious nature, **'An admirable evasion of whoremaster man, to lay his goatish disposition to the charge of a star!'** (*Act 1, Scene 2*) Shakespeare's use of **dramatic irony** is at its fullest with Edmund.

Edmund proves himself ambitious to the extent of laying false evidence that causes his brother to be hunted as an outlaw and betraying his father to torture and possible death. From his 'outcast' status at the start of the play, by the end of Act 3 he is Earl of Gloucester. He achieves all this by plotting and duplicity, pretending to Gloucester that he is reluctant to believe his brother could be planning to kill their father and to Edgar that **'I do serve you in this business'** (*Act 1, Scene 2*). He is clever enough to make his lies believable. Edmund's plan works so well that, not only does he get rid of Edgar, but he earns the praise and admiration of his father and the Duke of Cornwall in the process. Cornwall tells him, **'Natures of such deep trust we shall much need'** and Edmund pledges to serve him (*Act 2, Scene 1*).

---

dramatic irony when the audience knows something that the characters do not

machiavellian someone who is cunning, manipulative and deceitful; after the 15th-century political advisor Niccolo Machiavelli, who guided princes in how to maintain order and their own power by unscrupulous methods

Edmund, played by Simon Manyonda, brandishing the forged but fateful letter, in the 2016 Old Vic production

Gloucester's affection and trust is such that he reveals to Edmund his contact with the French and his aid for Lear. Edmund uses this to his own advantage, passing the information to Cornwall and then leaving the castle with Goneril before Gloucester is arrested. Even when he has the title he coveted, the audience is told by Regan, 'Edmund, I think, is gone, / In pity of his misery, to dispatch / His nighted life' (*Act 4, Scene 5*). His behaviour towards his father is similar to that of Goneril and Regan towards Lear.

Edmund's motive appears to be cynical self-interest and high ambition. He shows no emotion and has no compassion for his victims. Apart from a brief appearance in Act 4, Scene 2, the next time we see him he is commanding the English army, under Albany. He plots to use Albany to win the battle and allow one or other sister to murder her sibling and Albany. Then he will take the surviving sister. He plans the deaths of Lear and Cordelia, and the audience assumes his intention is to take the throne for himself.

Audiences are often puzzled as to why Edmund sends help to Lear and Cordelia when he does. One possible answer is given by J. Stampfer in his essay 'The Catharsis of King Lear', 1960, in which he indicates the point in the play at which Edmund acts. It follows the discovery of Goneril and Regan's bodies and prompts Edmund's comment, 'Yet Edmund was belov'd: / The one the other poison'd for my sake, / And after slew herself' (*Act 5, Scene 3*). The notion that he was loved (whether accurate or not) seems to stir something in him and he says, 'some good I mean to do / Despite of mine own nature' (*Act 5, Scene 3*). Right up to his death, Edmund remains aware of his own character and failings – an honesty about himself that draws the audience in, regardless of the evil he does.

Activity 3

a) Find three quotations that support each of the following statements:

- Edmund is ruthless and ambitious.
- Edmund resents his status as a bastard.
- Edmund plots to take what he wants.
- Edmund has self-knowledge that he shares with the audience.

b) Discuss whether or not you agree with J. Stampfer's assessment of why Edmund tries to save Lear and Cordelia.

Edgar

Edgar is a mysterious character. We see him only (as himself) with Edmund, who is manipulating him in the early part of the play. Edmund calls Edgar 'a brother noble, / Whose nature is so far from doing harms / That he suspects none; on whose foolish honesty / My practices ride easy!' (*Act 1, Scene 2*). Like his father, Edgar is credulous and suffers as a result.

He spends a large part of the play as Poor Tom, in which role he takes over from the Fool in looking after Lear. His disguise and the madness he utters seem to drive Lear over the edge. The character of Poor Tom represents the chaos brought by Lear on his kingdom. This is symbolized by the storm from which Poor Tom appears, almost as if summoned by Lear's address to 'poor naked wretches' (*Act 3, Scene 4*).

Lear identifies Poor Tom with himself, insisting that 'nothing could have subdu'd nature / To such a lowness but his unkind daughters' (*Act 3, Scene 4*), and refuses to seek shelter until Poor Tom is allowed to go with him. Gillian Woods, in her online article for the British Library 'King Lear: madness, the Fool and Poor Tom' (2013), says that the figure of Poor Tom, with its fractured identity composed of human, animal and demon, makes Lear feel his own frailty: 'Through Lear's madness, and through Edgar's pretence of madness, the tragedy insists on a common humanity'.

When Kent and the Fool take Lear off to Dover, Poor Tom takes on a new role as a guide for his blind father. One of the play's puzzles is why Edgar delays revealing his identity to Gloucester, even after he discovers his father knows the truth about him and Edmund. Edgar may have several reasons, including an understandable wish to punish his father a little for the way he was treated. He may also feel that he can prevent Gloucester's desire for suicide and teach him acceptance better in the role of an impartial guide than as the son he has wronged. In his introduction to the Arden edition (1966), Kenneth Muir says, 'There is, too, a suggestion that Edgar wished to rehabilitate himself in the eyes of the world, and punish Edmund, before revealing himself'. Edgar does admit that he waited too long, saying, 'Never – O fault! – reveal'd myself unto him, / Until some half-hour past, when I was arm'd' (*Act 5, Scene 3*).

At the start of the play Edgar seemed to be a good, but over-trusting heir to Gloucester. As Poor Tom, he sees the worst excesses of a fragmented kingdom and the nature of human cruelty. At times, he seems moral, as when he tells the audience in an aside, 'Why I do trifle thus with his despair / Is done to cure it' (*Act 4, Scene 6*). For an Elizabethan audience, suicide – the sin of despair that meant you had lost hope in God's mercy – signified you could no longer repent and were destined for hell. At the end of the play, having helped to save the king and having rescued and redeemed his father, Edgar is a worthy champion to fight for the cause of a reunited Britain.

The final words of the play (sometimes ascribed to Albany) are given to Edgar, now about to become king. His pilgrimage of suffering will help him to understand the need for justice and compassion that Lear realized too late.

Activity 4

a) Look at the statements below and put them in order of importance, giving your reasons and supporting them with textual evidence.

- Edgar will eventually take over as king.
- Edgar/Poor Tom represents the chaos in the kingdom, symbolized by the storm.
- Edgar's role as Poor Tom causes Lear to reflect on the injustices of his domain.
- Edgar is responsible for the safety and guidance of his father.
- Edgar is the champion who kills his brother and restores order to the country.

b) Discuss whether you think the following quotation makes Edgar appear just and moral, or rather puritanical:

The gods are just, and of our pleasant vices

Make instruments to plague us;

The dark and vicious place where thee he got

Cost him his eyes.

(*Edgar, Act 5, Scene 3 lines 159-62*)

Goneril and Regan

Goneril is Lear's eldest daughter and married to the Duke of Albany, whom she despises, while Regan, his second daughter, is wife to the Duke of Cornwall. Goneril is the first to agree to Lear's charade at the beginning, 'Sir, I love you more than word can wield the matter'. Regan follows and tries to outdo Goneril in hyperbole, showing the audience the competitive nature of the two women. As soon as Lear leaves the stage, the sisters confer on what they will have to put up with from him and 'the unruly waywardness that infirm and choleric years bring with them' (*Act 1, Scene 1*).

Once Goneril and Regan have divided the kingdom between them, Lear announces his intention of staying with each of them for a month at a time, taking his followers with him. There is some reason for Goneril's behaviour – an extra hundred men living under her roof, but not subject to 'house rules', might try anyone's patience. Goneril is presented as a slightly more sympathetic character at this stage, although encouraging her servants to **'Put on what weary negligence you please'** in order to anger Lear and drive him out of her house is provocative (*Act 1, Scene 3*).

Goneril seems to have a confidant rather than a servant in Oswald for she confides in him, calling her father an old fool and saying he should be ignored. She may be prepared for Lear's outburst when she requests that he **'A little to disquantity your train'**, which brings down the most shocking curses on her (*Act 1, Scene 4*). She tells her husband, **'Never afflict yourself to know more of it'**, as one might dismiss a child in a tantrum (*Act 1, Scene 4*). Lear departs to go to Regan, despite the Fool's warning, **'She will taste as like this as a crab does to a crab'** (*Act 1, Scene 5*).

The sisters are united against their father's desire to keep all the respect and obedience due to the king and a father while behaving like neither. Shakespeare presents them as having some cause for their behaviour, but it is notable that Lear does not curse Regan as he does Goneril, even though she tells him, **'I pray you, father, being weak, seem so'** (*Act 2, Scene 4*). Having tasted power, they gradually strip down Lear's authority until he is left with nothing. They make no attempt to dissuade him from going out into the storm. In fact Goneril tells Gloucester, **'My Lord, entreat him by no means to stay'** and Regan seems to be in accord (*Act 2, Scene 4*).

Goneril upbraids and torments her father; Jada Alberts and Tom E. Lewis in the Barbican Theatre production in 2016

As the play continues, the sisters' cruelty is made more obvious, especially in their treatment of Gloucester. It is Goneril who first suggests, 'Pluck out his eyes' (*Act 3, Scene 7*), but it's left to Regan and Cornwall to pursue this horrible course. The two sisters both believe themselves in love with Edmund, which creates a rift between them that quickly becomes bitter. Shakespeare first presents this when Edmund escorts Goneril home from Gloucester's castle. She sends Edmund back to Cornwall, saying she will 'give the distaff / Into my husband's hands' and tells him he will soon get 'A mistress's command', giving him a kiss (*Act 4, Scene 2*). Goneril's contempt for her husband is returned by Albany, who tells her 'You are not worth the dust which the rude wind / Blows in your face' (*Act 4, Scene 2*).

Meanwhile the now widowed Regan, distrusted with Edmund by Goneril, confides to Oswald that she is plotting to murder Gloucester whilst trying to get information from the steward about Goneril's letter to Edmund. She tells him bluntly, 'Edmund and I have talk'd / And more convenient is he for my hand / Than for your lady's' (*Act 4, Scene 5*). The audience later discovers that the letter contains directions for Edmund to murder Albany. As both sisters progress from their plan to kill Lear, through plans to dispose of Gloucester and Albany, they become deadly rivals. There is a poetic justice in their ends – Regan poisoned by Goneril, who then commits suicide, not through remorse but from a wish to avoid being hanged for plotting her husband's death. As the dying Edmund reflects, 'I was contracted to them both: all three / Now marry in an instant' (*Act 5, Scene 3*).

Activity 5

Discuss in what ways Edmund is similar to Goneril and Regan, and in what ways (apart from gender) he is different. Do you have any sympathy for any of these characters? Why or why not?

Cordelia

Lear's youngest and favourite daughter is Cordelia, with whom her father has planned to spend his retirement. When she is unable to comply with his unreasonable demand for a public declaration of love, he denounces her in front of the court, casts her off as his daughter and strips her of her dowry. As soon as she has heard Goneril's speech, Cordelia tells the audience in an aside, 'What shall Cordelia speak? Love, and be silent' (*Act 1, Scene 1*). Revealing that she does love her father and that 'my love's / More ponderous than my tongue' creates sympathy for her among the audience. It is a contrast with her sisters' easy and clearly hypocritical sentiments, and makes Lear's blindness to the truth more obvious.

Her answer to Lear is direct when he expects her to outdo her sisters: 'Nothing, my lord' (*Act 1, Scene 1*). She can say nothing that would go beyond what they have said and be truthful. Shakespeare presents her as honest but also as one who 'cannot heave / My heart into my mouth' (*Act 1, Scene 1*). She loves him as a daughter should love a father, 'no more nor less'. Cordelia is not shy – she states her position clearly and includes her opinion of her sisters. She also defends herself before her suitors to clarify that her only fault has been refusing to flatter her father. Cordelia can be seen as stubborn, like her father, and she certainly has no time for Goneril and Regan, sarcastically calling them 'The jewels of our father' and telling them, 'I know you what you are' (*Act 1, Scene 1*).

In spite of his treatment of her, Cordelia raises an army in France to come to Lear's rescue. He refuses to meet her because he is ashamed of his behaviour, but Cordelia has conferred with a doctor on how to cure his madness and watches over him while he sleeps. When he wakes, he imagines her as 'a soul in bliss' – a reference to heaven – and himself in hell, 'bound / Upon a wheel of fire' (*Act 4, Scene 7*). He imagines too, when he remembers her sisters' behaviour, that Cordelia will want him dead, with more cause. Cordelia's forgiving nature is shown in her cry, 'No cause, no cause' (*Act 4, Scene 7*).

Cordelia says remarkably little after her reunion with her father. The audience hears a report of her emotions when she learns of Lear's condition, but aside from reassuring him that she intends him no harm, her only short speech is to say that she feels more upset for Lear than for herself at losing the battle.

Cordelia has been compared to a Christ-figure in religious interpretations of the play, but she doesn't redeem anyone. She is certainly a victim and a symbol of goodness and love, especially compared with her sisters, but her death is so shocking and unnecessary that the play was considered 'unperformable' for many years (see the Performance chapter).

A feminist reading of the play would see Cordelia as at the mercy of powerful men. She is 'on the market' for a husband and the removal of her dowry means she is lucky that France sees her true merit and wants her without the traditional dowry. Cordelia, who began the play by being unable to speak for reasons of integrity, has her voice strangled for good in prison. Her wheel has gone full circle from 'Nothing' and silence in Act 1, Scene 1 to silence and nothing.

The Fool

Elizabethan fools were court jesters, privileged entertainers whose job was to tell the truth, indirectly, to those in power and remind them of their mortality. They had to tread a fine line as their masters could turn on them if they felt they were going too far.

The Fool in *King Lear* seems to be close to his master as he calls him 'nuncle' and is addressed by Lear as 'boy'. We are also told that, since Cordelia left for France 'the fool hath much pined away' (*Act 1, Scene 4*). The Fool's truth-telling gives him common ground with Cordelia and he asks Lear, 'Can you make use of nothing, nuncle?' (*Act 1, Scene 4*). He receives a similar answer to Cordelia – 'nothing can be made out nothing' – but turns it back on Lear – 'so much the rent of his land comes to' (*Act 1, Scene 4*). He continues the theme when he refers to Goneril's treatment of Lear:

Key quotation

I am better than thou art now; I am a fool, thou art nothing (*Act 1, Scene 4*).

When the Fool tells Lear, 'Thou should'st not have been old till thou hadst been wise', Lear acknowledges it by begging the Fool, 'Keep me in temper; I would not be mad!' (*Act 1, Scene 5*). The Fool follows Lear out into the storm and stays at his side when his knights seem to disappear. He tries to persuade the king, as he becomes madder, to seek shelter and he tries to prevent Lear taking off his clothes in imitation of Poor Tom, 'Prithee, nuncle, be contented; 'tis a naughty night to swim in' (*Act 3, Scene 4*).

The Fool's last words are 'And I'll go to bed at noon' (*Act 3, Scene 6*), in answer to Lear's comment about having supper in the morning, and the audience's final glimpse of him is helping Kent and Gloucester to move the sleeping Lear in preparation for a journey to Dover. His disappearance from the play, apparently without explanation, has created much comment. His role lessens as Lear goes mad and he can no longer prevent it. In performance terms, he is probably needed as a different character (possibly Cordelia) and the audience may find their own explanation.

The Fool, played by Graham Turner, entertains Lear and his entourage in the Royal Shakespeare Company production in 2016

Activity 6

In Act 5, Scene 3, Lear says, **'And my poor fool is hang'd!'**.

a) Discuss whether this remark is intended to refer to Cordelia or to the possible fate of the Fool earlier in the play.

b) Are there any ways in which Cordelia and the Fool are alike? You could consider:

- their love for Lear
- the way they both tell him the truth
- their absence from parts of the play.

Kent

The Earl of Kent is the other character who speaks the truth to Lear. His spirited defence of Cordelia is combined with his fear for Lear's safety if he gives power to her sisters: **'What would'st thou do, old man? Think'st thou that duty shall have dread to speak / When power to flattery bows?'** (*Act 1, Scene 1*) His intervention provokes Lear, who banishes his most loyal friend.

Kent's loyalty proves steadfast as he returns in disguise to serve the king, despite his poor treatment. At Gloucester's castle, Kent quarrels again with Oswald, who refuses to fight him. We later learn that Oswald interrupted the message Kent was carrying from the king to Regan, and caused her and Cornwall to depart at once, telling Kent to go with them. Kent is put in the stocks, although he protests that such treatment of the king's messenger dishonours the king himself. He is a bluff soldier rather than a courtier and seems almost as quick to anger as Lear himself. While in the stocks, the audience discovers he has been in touch with Cordelia and has a letter from her. In fact Kent seems to have a network of spies that keep him informed of events. He is kept abreast of affairs throughout the kingdom and in France, and tells one of Lear's followers that **'from France there comes a power / Into this scatter'd kingdom'** and sends him to Dover to find Cordelia and give her his ring (*Act 3, Scene 1*).

In keeping with his role as intelligence gatherer, it is Kent who discovers the return of the French army to his own country and how Cordelia received the letters telling her of Lear's situation. When he does meet with Cordelia, she urges him to put off his disguise. His answer is rather mysterious – **'Yet to be known shortens my made intent'** (*Act 4, Scene 7*) – and we wonder what he's waiting for. By the time he does decide to speak out, Lear is grieving over the dead Cordelia and has little interest in Kent or even the fate of Goneril and Regan. It is the true friend Kent who tells Edgar, **'Vex not his ghost: O! let him pass; he hates him / That would upon the rack** of this tough world / Stretch him out longer' (Act 5, Scene 3). He dismisses the notion of ruling alongside Edgar, saying, 'I have a journey, sir, shortly to go; / My master calls me, I must not say no' (*Act 5, Scene 3*). The most loyal friend through his lifetime proposes to follow his king even after death.

Activity 7

Write a short monologue for each of the following characters: Cordelia, Kent and the Fool, explaining to the audience why they think that telling the truth is so important that they will risk everything for it.

Oswald

Oswald is Goneril's servant but he also aspires to be a gentleman for he wears a sword, although it is noticeable that he only uses it once. He is in his mistress's confidence as she entrusts him to write letters to her sister. He appears to be steward to the household and is ambitious to climb higher.

Oswald is good at being ill-mannered, as Kent describes how he interrupted his meeting with Regan and Cornwall, and it is thanks to him that Kent ends up in the stocks, a severe insult to the king he represents. Of course, a true gentleman would have drawn his sword and fought Kent on equal terms, but Oswald is presented as a social climber who screams for help instead. The only time he draws a weapon is to murder blind old Gloucester and then Edgar forces him to fight and kills him instead.

At no point does Oswald hesitate to carry out the sisters' worst commands, never mind remonstrate them with them about their evil deeds. In this respect he is contrasted with Gloucester's servant, who remonstrates with Cornwall over the blinding and then kills him, giving his own life in the process.

Writing about characterization and roles

When writing about characters it is important to look at their dialogue, their actions and the way others react to them. What their role is in the play and how well they fulfil it is also important. Remember to discuss the characters as constructs, created by Shakespeare for specific purposes, rather than as if they are real people. You need to include detailed analysis, supported by well-chosen textual evidence and some reference to the relevant views of literary critics, if you aspire to the higher grades.

Language

Blank verse and prose

Shakespeare writes mostly in blank verse, although he usually ends a scene on a **rhyming couplet**. The metre is iambic pentameter, which is like the human heartbeat. It would soon get dull if this metre was exactly followed, so some lines may have more or fewer syllables or the punctuation may cause the stress to fall differently. For example, in Act 1, Scene 1, 'Meantime, we shall express our darker purpose' has an extra syllable, while the lines 'Unburthen'd crawl towards death. Our son of Cornwall, / And you, our no less loving son of Albany' contain a **caesura** followed by **enjambment**, which alters the rhythm of the verse.

> **caesura** a stop within the line itself, as opposed to an end-stopped line
>
> **enjambment** the continuation of a sentence, running one line onto the next
>
> **rhyming couplet** two lines that rhyme on the last syllable of each

Activity 1

Look at Lear's speech from Act 1, Scene 1 beginning, 'Meantime, we shall express our darker purpose'.

a) Read the speech aloud just for the metre, stressing alternate syllables and noting where they differ from a strict iambic pentameter.

b) Read it aloud, using the punctuation to judge how to give meaning to the words. Note how often this means pausing in mid-line and running across the lines to make sense of the words.

c) Discuss and make notes on how the rhythm and flow of the verse reflects the meanings of the lines, e.g. how the line above throws the emphasis on 'darker purpose', which has the double meaning of hidden and evil.

d) Analyse Lear's speech from Act 2, Scene 4 beginning, 'O, reason not the need!' in the same way.

e) Discuss the differences in tone and imagery of the two speeches and how Shakespeare reflects this in his use of verse.

In *King Lear*, as in all his plays, Shakespeare uses both prose and verse, often in the same scene. Some uses are clear. Blank verse is used for formal occasions such as the division of the kingdom in Act 1, Scene 1 and to express serious thoughts and ideas, as when Edmund is persuading Gloucester of Edgar's villainy in Act 2, Scene 1. It is also used when characters are speaking in their roles as nobles or rulers.

Prose is used for informal conversations, as between Kent and Gloucester at the start of the play and between Goneril and Regan at the end of Act 1, Scene 1. It is also used by those who do not have positions of power, such as the Fool, although the Fool also has snatches of doggerel verse and songs. Prose is used by mad characters as well, for whom verse would seem too ordered. When Edgar becomes Poor Tom, his verse-speaking changes to prose and the same happens to Lear as his wits desert him. Prose is also used for documents such as letters, which would sound rather odd written in verse.

Activity 2

Look at Act 1, Scene 1 and focus on Goneril and Regan, who both speak in verse and in prose.

a) Discuss how far the reasons for their speech and the person to whom they speak may affect their style of language.

b) Write a paragraph about Shakespeare's possible reasons for giving the sisters both verse and prose to speak in the same scene.

c) Find another scene where a character speaks in verse and prose, and discuss why Shakespeare might have done this.

Images and symbols

In his book *Shakespeare's Language* (2001), Frank Kermode points out the recurrent images and motifs of nothing, seeing and addition that permeate the play.

Nothing

The word 'nothing' appears first as Cordelia's answer to her sisters' insincerity in the first scene. It is repeated by Lear as a question and affirmed again by Cordelia. To that, Lear insists 'Nothing will come of nothing: speak again' (*Act 1, Scene 1*). The idea reappears in Gloucester's conversation with Edmund over the forged letter supposedly from Edgar. When Edmund answers 'Nothing, my lord' to Gloucester's request to know what he was reading, his father points out, 'The quality of nothing hath not such need to hide itself' (*Act 1, Scene 2*). In both scenes, the fathers are misled by their children's unwillingness to elaborate on 'nothing'. Lear misunderstands Cordelia's silence and Gloucester is deceived by Edmund's pretence. In both cases, what comes from 'nothing' is a chain of events that destroys both fathers and a kingdom.

Lear has a similar conversation with the Fool, who asks him, referring to his land division, 'Can you make no use of nothing, nuncle?' Lear tells him, 'nothing can be made out of nothing' (*Act 1, Scene 4*). Just as Cordelia received no land for her 'nothing', so Lear no longer has land or power, and therefore has nothing. The Fool also points out, 'I would not be thee, nuncle; thou hast pared thy wit o'both sides, and left nothing i'th'middle' (*Act 1, Scene 4*). The Fool is unsparing in reminding Lear that he has given everything away and is left with nothing.

When Edgar becomes Poor Tom as a result of Edmund's machinations, he describes how he will disguise himself and finishes his soliloquy, **'Edgar I nothing am'** (*Act 2, Scene 3*). This suggests that, in adopting the persona of a bedlam beggar, the earl's son has reduced himself to nothing. What comes from his 'nothing' is a stronger character, one able to help the king, to give aid and spiritual comfort to his father, and finally to become champion over Edmund and the next king of Britain.

The ending of the play, brings home cruelly the idea that nothing has truly come of nothing. It was Lear who needed to think again.

Lear contemplating, perhaps on whether his crown is worth anything or nothing, played by Ian Holm in the BBC production in 1997

Activity 3

Look at the end of play. Just before Lear dies in Act 5, Scene 3, he utters the line, **'Never, never, never, never, never!'**

a) Discuss how this line, and the ending of the play itself, reflects the recurring imagery of 'nothing' that runs through the whole text.

b) Create a spider diagram to show the way this linguistic idea is used through the text.

Sight and seeing

The symbolic imagery of sight and seeing is a strong thread that connects ideas throughout the play. In a prophetic phrase, Goneril declares she loves Lear 'dearer than eye-sight' (*Act 1, Scene 1*), among other precious things. Lear's inability to see through her rhetoric and that of Regan, and his lack of insight into Cordelia's truth, is reflected in his treatment of Kent, whom he banishes 'Out of my sight!' and who retorts, 'See better, Lear; and let me still remain / The true blank of thine eye' (*Act 1, Scene 1*). The implication that Kent is the one who sees clearly and should be listened to goes unheeded by the king, who cannot look beyond his own vanity and gratification. He sees nothing where he should perceive truth and loyalty.

Lear's moral blindness is paralleled by Gloucester, who demands of Edmund, 'Let's see, let's see', and, in reading the letter in Act 1, Scene 2, is unable to see that it is a libel on his elder son and that he is being hoodwinked. When Lear discovers Goneril is beginning to use the power he has given her against him, he feels to be not himself, demanding, 'Does Lear walk thus? speak thus? Where are his eyes?' (*Act 1, Scene 4*). The suggestion is that he cannot believe his eyes that his daughter is giving commands to her father. When his dreadful curse fails to move her, he weeps tears of anger and frustration but then rallies, saying, 'Old fond eyes, / Beweep this cause again, I'll pluck ye out' (*Act 1, Scene 4*).

Meanwhile Edmund is staging a drama for his father's benefit, where he will see for himself Edgar's 'treachery'. Gloucester, as expected, sees what Edmund tells him to and promptly outlaws his loyal son. With both fathers now having banished the wrong child, the Fool tells Kent, 'All that follow their noses are led by their eyes but blind men; and there's not a nose among twenty but can smell him that's stinking' (*Act 2, Scene 4*). He is suggesting that Kent is unwise to follow one who stinks of Fortune's displeasure (Lear) when only fools will stay.

Following the scene of the mock trial of Goneril and Regan, the 'pelican daughters' (*Act 3, Scene 4*), as Lear has come to see them, is the terrible scene of Gloucester's blinding. Gloucester himself, all unaware, says he has sent the king to Dover 'Because I would not see / Thy cruel nails pluck out his poor old eyes', to which Cornwall replies, 'See't shalt thou never' (*Act 3, Scene 7*), as he destroys one of Gloucester's eyes.

Act 4, Scene 6, in which Edgar pretends to his father that he has reached the top of a cliff in Dover, is particularly rich in imagery to do with sight. Edgar's pretended description of the clifftop uses phrases to do with seeing – 'cast one's eyes so low, appear like mice, too small for sight' (*Act 4, Scene 6*) – but also phrases to do with the inner eye, or imagination, something in which Gloucester is deficient. When the mad Lear enters, much of his dialogue is to do with eyes and sight. He tells Gloucester, 'No eyes in your head, nor no money in your purse? Your eyes are in a heavy case, your purse in a light: yet you see how this world goes' (*Act 4, Scene 6*). Gloucester replies, 'I see it feelingly'. For both old men, the loss of wits and eyes have brought a kind of wisdom and moral vision that they lacked before.

Activity 4

The symbolism of sight and blindness has several layers of meaning. It can refer to physical states as in Gloucester's case, to human character as both Lear and Gloucester demonstrate, to moral consequences and to spiritual states.

a) Find some of these important symbols and images in the play and discuss which category or categories they fit.

b) Then complete a table like the one below with your views and evidence.

Example	Physical	Character	Moral	Spiritual

Addition

Frank Kermode also comments on Shakespeare's use of the term 'addition', which he sees as being applied to titles and lands but also to such things as clothes and servants. When Lear announces his decision to give away his kingdom, he intends to keep 'The name and all th'addition to a king' (Act 1, Scene 1). As Shakespeare later shows, this includes a hundred knights and the right to treat his daughters' houses and servants as his own. The stripping away of these 'additions' reveals Lear's lack of power.

The calculation with which Lear arranged the bargaining of speeches of love in exchange for land is repeated against him by the two sisters. They coldly bargain down the number of 'additions' to his train that they are prepared to have in their houses until Regan's 'What need one?' This provokes the outburst of, 'O, reason not the need!', followed by a speech in which Lear points out that without the additions that make a person human, their life would be 'cheap as beast's' (Act 2, Scene 4). He points out that the sisters' clothes are not made just for warmth but for show.

By the time the harsh weather, the chaos in his mind and the entrance of Poor Tom have sent him to the edge of madness, Lear realizes that, under the additions, 'unaccommodated man is no more but such a poor, bare, forked animal as thou art' (Act 3, Scene 4). He tears off his own clothes, which he now sees as 'lendings' (Act 3, Scene 4), which suggests that he sees his kingly additions as borrowed robes.

Activity 5

Write one or two paragraphs, describing what you consider to be Shakespeare's views on 'addition', giving evidence for your ideas.

Foolishness

A lesser, but still significant image through the play is that of foolishness. In Act 1, Scene 1, it is Kent who points out, 'To plainness honour's bound / When majesty falls to folly'. When Kent is banished, the Fool becomes instrumental in making Lear see his own folly. He does this with a mixture of jokes and mysterious sayings and verses. He has more licence for this than the other characters and is the only one who would get away with suggesting that Lear had made his daughters into his mothers: 'thou gav'st them the rod and putt'st down thine own breeches' (*Act 1, Scene 4*).

The bad children see their fathers as fools. Edmund refers to his 'credulous father' and Edgar's 'foolish honesty' (*Act 1, Scene 2*), implying that to be trusting is to be stupid (which future events confirm), while Goneril tells Oswald, 'Old fools are babes again, and must be us'd / With checks as flatteries, when they are seen abus'd' (*Act 1, Scene 3*). The Fool also tells Lear, 'thou would'st make a good fool' (*Act 1, Scene 5*), before pointing out that his age has not brought wisdom.

Nature and animal imagery

These are some of the powerful recurring images in the play. The natural order of things, as seen by Shakespeare's audience, with the king in control of the country and the father in control of the family, is disrupted. The result is that those with bestial instincts are given control and the animal rules of 'kill or be killed' prevail.

Goneril is referred to as a serpent several times by Lear and Albany, and she and Regan are compared to adders by Edmund. These images allude to the serpent that represents evil in the biblical story of Adam and Eve, where Eve allegedly caused the downfall of Man. They are also called vultures, wolves, tigers and sharks – all predators that kill to survive.

In his first soliloquy, Edmund says, 'Thou, Nature, art my goddess; to thy law / My services are bound' and claims that he follows the rules of the natural universe rather than the natural duty of son to father (*Act 1, Scene 2*). This imagery is layered since, being illegitimate, he is his father's natural, rather than lawful son. He seems to think that this absolves him from any moral duty towards his father or his brother and gives him the right to use his native cunning to get what he can.

This view of what is natural in relationships – the duty of a parent to guide their children and the duty of children to love and obey their father – is set against the view of what is natural in the universe – the weather and the behaviour of animals. When the natural human order, represented by the rule of law, is overturned, the moral order breaks down and 'Man's life is cheap as beast's' (*Act 2, Scene 4*).

When Edmund tells Gloucester that he refused to help Edgar in 'his unnatural purpose' (*Act 2, Scene 1*), the irony comes not merely from Edmund ascribing his own ambition to his brother but from what the audience already knows of his views on nature. When he is finally defeated by Edgar, the lawful brother asserts his natural right: 'I am no less in blood than thou art, Edmund; / If more, the more th'hast wronged me' (*Act 5, Scene 3*).

The natural world is seen to reflect the human one as Lear's struggle to retain his reason, and the chaos in his mind, as in his kingdom, is reflected by the storm. The speech he directs at the elements is one of the finest in the play and worth examining as an example of Shakespeare's poetic technique.

Activity 6

Read the speech beginning **'Blow, winds, and crack your cheeks!'** from Act 3, Scene 2 aloud.

a) Find examples of each of the following:

- personification
- hyphenated adjectives
- violent words and phrases
- onomatopoeia

b) Discuss the effects created by these techniques.

c) Write a paragraph giving your views about how Shakespeare's language reflects meaning in this speech.

When a person is pared down to their basics, whether through physical or mental suffering, their essential humanity is lost. When Lear enters with Cordelia's body, he howls like an animal in pain and such grief can find relief only in death as a final release from suffering.

Tips for assessment

One way of gaining a higher grade is to show your understanding of the way in which the play contains echoes and repetitions of language that connect themes, motifs and ideas. The use of symbols and recurring images is important in reinforcing these to an audience that is watching and listening rather than reading the text.

Language and character

The way a character speaks is very important in defining their personality and role for an audience. The manner in which Lear changes throughout the play is reflected in his use of language. In Act 1, Scene 1, he starts speaking with an autocratic tone of command, using the royal 'we'. It is highly formal and ceremonious, e.g. **'Know that we have divided / In three our kingdom'**. At the same time, it is couched in terms of material advantage and bargaining: **'Which of you shall we say doth love us most?'**. He asks Cordelia, **'what can you say to draw / A third more opulent than your sisters?'** Her suitors are described in terms of what their lands produce – **'vines of France and milk of Burgundy'** – and later in the scene he says **'her price is fallen'**. When he is crossed or disappointed, his language becomes intemperate and disproportionate to the events: **'Here I disclaim all my paternal care, / Propinquity and property of blood, / And as a stranger to my heart and me / Hold thee from this for ever'**.

Activity 7

a) Discuss and comment on what each of the following quotations suggests about the character of Lear in Act 1, Scene 1. Copy and complete the table below.

Quotation	What it suggests about Lear
Know that we have divided / In three our kingdom	
Which of you shall we say doth love us most?	
what can you say to draw / A third more opulent than your sisters?	
vines of France and milk of Burgundy	
Here I disclaim all my paternal care, / Propinquity and property of blood, / And as a stranger to my heart and me / Hold thee from this for ever.	

b) Write three sentences giving your views on how the language used by Cordelia and France provides a different viewpoint from that used by Lear and Burgundy.

When he begins to feel the loss of his power, Lear's language uses symbolic metaphors to express how he blames himself: 'Beat at this gate, that let thy folly in, / And thy dear judgment out!' (*Act 1, Scene 4*). He uses shocking language to Goneril in cursing her as a potential mother. Unlike the first scene, his frustration is expressed in 'these hot tears' and the conviction that Regan will take his part, 'with her nails / She'll flay thy wolfish visage' (*Act 1, Scene 4*).

The king of France values Cordelia for herself rather than for her lost dowry, whereas Lear measures her worth in flatteries; Natalie Simpson and Marcus Griffiths in the 2016 Royal Shakespeare Company production

His language expresses rage at his impotence but it seems to beat itself out against the storm. The line, **'I am a man / More sinn'd against than sinning'**, marks a turning point as he shows concern for the Fool: **'I have one part in my heart / That's sorry yet for thee'** (*Act 3, Scene 2*). Instead of wanting the storm to eradicate the earth, he now realizes its effects on **'Poor naked wretches'** and his language begins to reflect his previous lack of justice and care for the poor of his kingdom (*Act 3, Scene 4*). It also reflects his increasing madness as he meets Poor Tom. In the later scenes, his madness uses the language of sexual disgust, perhaps commenting on what procreation has led to in his daughters. It also reflects the theme of justice as he talks of how the rich and powerful bend justice to their will against the poor.

Activity 8

a) Discuss how Shakespeare uses language to present the various stages of Lear's journey towards redemption and death.

b) Create a flow diagram like the one below to show each stage, appropriate quotations and evaluations of each quotation. For example:

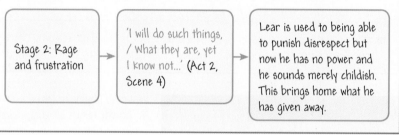

Stage 2: Rage and frustration → 'I will do such things, / What they are, yet I know not...' (Act 2, Scene 4) → Lear is used to being able to punish disrespect but now he has no power and he sounds merely childish. This brings home what he has given away.

Kent and Cordelia

These two characters both use language that reflects their honesty and plain speaking, and both of them suffer for it. Their journeys through the play seem to be linked. In the first scene, Cordelia tells Lear she lacks **'that glib and oily art / To speak and purpose not'**, implying that her sisters both possess this (*Act 1, Scene 1*). Kent dares to say to Lear, **'I'll tell thee thou dost evil'**. Both Cordelia and Kent are banished for their pains, although Kent's loyalty brings him back in disguise. His appearance may be different, but his **idiolect** doesn't change.

idiolect an individual person or character's way of speaking

The language Kent uses to Oswald produces some of the most colourful cursing in the play: 'Thou whoreson zed! thou unnecessary letter!' (*Act 2, Scene 2*) He adds to the animal imagery by comparing Oswald with a rat and a dog and, when Cornwall dislikes his plain talking, he shows an unexpected ability to use the tone of a courtier. This is undoubtedly sarcastic and Kent makes it worse by saying that it is his going 'out of my dialect' that offends the duke.

Cordelia is forthright in her expressions of sorrow for Lear's state when they meet again. She too uses the imagery of animals when she says, 'Mine enemy's dog, / Though he had bit me, should have stood that night / Against my fire' (*Act 4, Scene 7*). She reassures her penitent father that she has no cause to hate him. Her last words on stage are to say, 'For thee, oppressed king, I am cast down; / Myself could else out-frown false Fortune's frown' (*Act 5, Scene 3*).

The Fool and Poor Tom

Both characters speak in riddles and are difficult to understand. The Fool speaks in this way because it enables him to tell the truth without being too blunt (unlike Kent). He calls Lear a fool on several occasions and reminds him what he has done in giving away his kingdom. He uses doggerel verses and snatches of song to reinforce his point. He blames Lear for the state he is in, telling his master he is 'Lear's shadow' (*Act 1, Scene 4*), and comparing Goneril to a cuckoo fed by a sparrow, which bites off its 'parent's' head. His loyalty to Lear is shown in Kent's report that he is Lear's only companion in the storm and 'labours to out-jest / His heart-strook injuries' (*Act 3, Scene 1*). That is the only way he knows how to speak to his master.

Edgar's language changes dramatically when he becomes Poor Tom. Shakespeare uses soliloquy to tell the audience that Edgar proposes 'To take the basest and most poorest shape / That ever penury, in contempt of man, / brought near to beast' (*Act 2, Scene 3*). Such a disguise requires the language of lunacy and Edgar shows himself surprisingly well-acquainted with the names of fiends. In an article on the British Library website, Gillian Woods says:

His disguise is peculiarly multiple: the actor playing this role is Edgar and Poor Tom and the devils possessing Poor Tom. This fracturing of identity into different parts is evident as Poor Tom's language slips into different voices: 'Beware my follower. Peace, Smulkin, peace, thou fiend!' (*Act 3, Scene 4*). The Fool's privileged voice enables him to critique the king. But Poor Tom's language is so madly and maddeningly open in its address that it too might be describing Lear or even the audience, as well as Edgar and Poor Tom.

(Gillian Woods, *King Lear: madness, the Fool and Poor Tom*, 2013)

Small wonder that Gloucester fails to recognize him. He abandons this form of speech when he becomes his blind father's guide, for Gloucester comments, **'Methinks thy voice is alter'd, and thou speak'st / In better phrase and matter than thou didst'** (*Act 4, Scene 6*). Edgar seems to be an actor, for he changes his accent several times in his attempt to convince Gloucester that he has really fallen from a cliff. When we see him at the end of the play, his language has changed again, to a form suited to a future king: **'Conspirant 'gainst this high illustrious prince'** (*Act 5, Scene 3*).

The Fool, played by John Hurt in this 1983 TV production, speaks in riddles, doggerel and snatches of song to remind the king that he is but a man

Activity 9

a) Find three examples of each of the following:

- the Fool calling Lear a fool
- the Fool's use of verse and song
- the Fool trying to comfort Lear in the storm
- Edgar's use of mad talk to mirror Lear's situation
- Edgar's changes of tone when he and Gloucester arrive at Dover
- Edgar's formal and authoritative voice at the end of the play.

b) Use your examples to write a set of notes on how the language of Edgar and the Fool reflect their characters and roles in the play.

Goneril, Regan and Edmund

The play's evil characters are notable for their ability to use language to their own benefit. Frank Kermode points out that in the first scene of the play Goneril uses a form of rhetoric called 'the topic of inexpressibility'. This very formal method of praising a king uses the 'more-than-I-can-say' technique, e.g. 'more than word can wield the matter' (*Act 1, Scene 1*). She is followed by Regan using another rhetorical technique, that of the 'she's said everything I would say' but 'she comes too short' (*Act 1, Scene 1*). What this suggests is that the sisters are behaving as courtiers, rather than daughters. Having got what they want, their language changes instantly as they plot together: 'We must do something, and i'th'heat' (*Act 1, Scene 1*).

Goneril's language shows nothing but contempt for her father and her husband – for Lear because he is old and has no power left, and for Albany because he shows respect and compassion for Lear.

Regan's language reflects a similar attitude to her father, although Cornwall seems to have her respect, if not her love. By the end of the play, the two sisters are using the terms of jealousy to quarrel over Edmund.

Edmund uses the language of filial affection to disarm Gloucester and convince him of his own loyalty and Edgar's betrayal. Shakespeare uses dramatic irony in Edmund's soliloquies to show the audience that the terms he uses are a deception, designed to get him Gloucester's lands and title. His language changes only at his death, when he announces, 'some good I mean to do' (*Act 5, Scene 3*).

Activity 10

a) Which of these three characters says the following:

- Idle old man, / That still would manage those authorities/ That he hath given away!

- I see the business. / Let me, if not by birth, have lands by wit: / All with me's meet that I can fashion fit.

- I look'd not for you yet, nor am provided / For your fit welcome. Give ear, sir, to my sister

b) Discuss which words and phrases prompted your answer.

Writing about language

When you write about characters, you will gain higher marks for showing how Shakespeare uses their speech patterns and vocabulary to reflect their personalities. You will also gain marks for showing understanding of and evaluating their roles in the play as a whole.

Power and powerlessness

Power is at the core of the play and it relates to the theme of justice. The power of the ruler involves the Jacobean notion of the divine right of kings and the proper order of the Chain of Being. It is a power that brings responsibility, something that Lear shrugs off, only later realizing its essential importance. Without the power that ruling a united country gives him, he is only an old man making tiresome demands on his daughters.

It takes a very short time for him to realize this. Within two weeks of quartering himself and his hundred men with Goneril, she is complaining about him and them, and telling Oswald to treat Lear with rudeness, in the hope that he will depart for Regan's house. The audience heard the sisters planning to do something about Lear soon after he devolved his ruling position to them. Goneril tells Regan, 'Pray you, let us hit together: if our father carry authority with such disposition as he bears, this last surrender of his will but offend us' (Act 1, Scene 1). Shakespeare uses this dramatic irony to create anticipation of what will happen as the source of government changes.

As Lear's power wanes, so that of his daughters grows. He may rail against Goneril's request to 'disquantity your train' and even heap dreadful curses on her (Act 1, Scene 4), but while he lives with her, he cannot do anything except leave. Having banished the two most loyal people from his court, he is at the mercy of those to whom he gave his power – and they use it without scruple. Not until he is left without any of his followers except Kent and the Fool, and he is at the mercy of the storm, does Lear face what he has done.

At the moment when his rage and frustration exhausts itself on the heath he realizes what it is to be without influence. His own situation makes him aware of the desperate need of the 'Poor naked wretches' in his erstwhile kingdom (Act 3, Scene 4). As his wits slip from him, he comes to see how the rich and powerful organize society for their own benefit, while those without power are mistreated and unable even to complain. He feels compassion for the Fool, who has loyally followed him, despite threats of whipping – How dost, my boy? Art cold? (Act 3, Scene 2) – and regards Poor Tom's mad gabble as wisdom: 'Noble philosopher, your company' (Act 3, Scene 4).

In the storm, Lear, bereft of all power even over his own mind, encounters Gloucester, blinded because of his inability to tell which son loves him; Royal Shakespeare Company, 2010

Activity 1

Discuss the way in which Shakespeare uses irony to show Lear understanding the responsibility of power when he can no longer use it.

The exercise of power without responsibility or compassion results in a kingdom torn apart. Already divided by Lear's wilful decree, according to Kent, 'There is division, / Although as yet the face of it is cover'd / With mutual cunning, 'twixt Albany and Cornwall' *(Act 3, Scene 1)*. This comment both echoes and contrasts with Gloucester's first speech in the play to Kent: 'in the division of the kingdom, it appears not which of the dukes he values most' *(Act 1, Scene 1)*. The sisters, although they make common cause against their father, become deadly rivals in their desire for Edmund to the extent that Goneril comments, 'I had rather lose the battle than that sister / Should loosen him and me' *(Act 5, Scene 1)*, where the pun connects the losses as equal. The play presents a realm in disorder, where those in power are guided by their own self-interest and casual cruelty is commonplace.

When he is reunited with Cordelia, Lear finds that he can be happy even in a prison if he has his beloved daughter to comfort him. The discovery of the power of love and kindness is the result of suffering and loss. At the end of the play, when Albany offers his kingdom back, he is no longer interested in power.

Key quotation

There thou might'st behold
The great image of Authority:
A dog's obey'd in office
(Lear, Act 4, Scene 6)

In the subplot, power is gained by subterfuge and cunning rather than public hypocrisy and flattery. Edmund wins power over his father and brother by lying and driving a false wedge between them. He uses elaborate play-acting to convince Gloucester: 'It is his hand, my lord; but I hope his heart is not in the contents' *(Act 1, Scene 2)*. He then does the same with Edgar, using his brother's open and honest nature against him. Having won his father's trust, he gains more power by betraying him to Cornwall and being given the duke's title as a reward.

Edmund exerts authority over Goneril and Regan through his sexual charm and plays them off against each other in the hope of becoming king. Whereas the sisters are opportunists, seizing the chance that Lear gives them, Edmund creates his own chances. All three are unscrupulous in their taking and wielding of power.

Key quotation

Well, my legitimate, if this letter speed,
And my invention thrive, Edmund the base
Shall top th'legitimate
(Edmund, Act 1, Scene 2)

If those who have power abuse it, those without are shown to have love and kindness. The Fool tries to comfort Lear out on the heath; the banished Kent returns to serve Lear in his hour of need; Gloucester leaves his castle to find Lear shelter; Edgar as Poor Tom tries to help Lear and then saves his father from despair and suicide. In the subplot, Gloucester's servants try to help him – one even kills Cornwall in his defence – and one of his tenants guides him, at risk to himself.

It is a tribute to Shakespeare's depiction of universal humanity that modern audiences will also see how often those with power use it for their own ends, while there is often understanding and compassion from those who have least.

Key quotations

Gracious my lord, hard by here is a hovel;
Some friendship will it lend you 'gainst the tempest
(Kent, Act 3, Scene 2)
Prithee, nuncle, be contented; 'tis a naughty night to swim in.
(The Fool, Act 3, Scene 4)

As well as political power, Shakespeare also presents the audience with characters who have moral authority. This comes not from position or wealth but from an innate sense of what is right and just. It is not confined to any rank or class, but is shown by nobles – Cordelia, Edgar, Kent and Albany – and by those of lesser social status – the Fool, Gloucester's servant and his old tenant.

This kind of moral power, which comes ultimately from the desire to do good, shows itself in love, loyalty and compassion for others. Where political power, ambition and greed lead to chaos, moral power, kindness and generosity lead to harmony. All audiences will understand this concept and hope that moral power will win in the end.

Activity 2

a) Discuss the difference between political power and moral power.

- Which characters have political power and how do they use it? Does this change as the play progresses and, if so, how?
- Which characters have moral power and how do they use it? Does this change as the play progresses and, if so, how?

b) Write your findings in three paragraphs using evidence from the text.

Justice

Linked with the theme of power is that of justice. It was seen by Shakespeare's audience as a divine attribute but the gods in *King Lear* seem to ignore it for the most part. Lear himself, who should be the dispenser of justice in his kingdom, uses little of it in his dealings with his daughters and with Kent. The punishments suffered by Lear and Gloucester seem to be out of proportion to their offences, although it is hard to say whether anything less than the loss of everything, including his reason, would have made Lear see the effects of his rash decisions. The same is true of Gloucester, who is presented as morally blind until he loses his eyes and is told by Regan, 'it was he / That made the overture of thy treasons to us, / Who is too good to pity thee' (*Act 3, Scene 7*). He then realizes how Edmund has deceived him and that 'Edgar was abus'd' (*Act 3, Scene 7*). It is one of the many ironies Shakespeare uses in *King Lear* – and a metaphor taken from classical tragedy – that the blind Gloucester sees more clearly, just as Lear loses his reason, and discovers a deeper truth about the need for justice in an unjust world.

The idea that he has not been a provider of justice comes to Lear in the storm when he thinks of the poor without shelter and realizes, 'O, I have ta'en / Too little care of this!' (*Act 3, Scene 4*). In his book *Justice in King Lear* (1962), C.J. Sissons points out, 'No longer a king, no longer hedged about with divinity, a mere "idle old man" as Goneril puts it scornfully, he is the better able to examine kingship, the sanctions of royal power, and justice, with eyes no longer veiled by their exercise in his own person.'

Lear seems to believe in divine justice when, out in the storm, he calls on the gods who released the elements to direct them against those who pervert human justice, claiming, 'I am a man / More sinn'd against than sinning' (*Act 3, Scene 2*). His list includes those who hide their crimes and pretend to virtue, and it echoes Cordelia's words to her sisters in Act 1, Scene 1: 'Time shall unfold what plighted cunning hides; / Who covers faults, at last with shame derides'.

Gloucester, on the other hand, despairs of divine justice as he cries out, 'As flies to wanton boys, are we to th'gods; / They kill us for their sport' (*Act 4, Scene 1*). Not until Edgar tricks him into thinking he has been miraculously preserved does Gloucester resign himself to patience.

As C.J. Sisson points out, 'there is in fact poetic justice enough in *King Lear*'. Goneril poisons Regan and then stabs herself. Edmund is slain in a trial-by-combat by Edgar, the brother he tried to have executed. Cornwall is killed by one of Gloucester's servants, seeking to defend his master against gratuitous cruelty, and Oswald is killed by Gloucester's legitimate son as he tries to murder the old man. For Lear and Gloucester, the hardships and grief brought about by their own faults finally cause them to die from an excess of emotion that stops their hearts – joy in the case of Gloucester and grief in the case of Lear.

For Cordelia, there is no justice – not from her father at the start of the play nor from the gods at the end. This is what makes the ending so hard to bear. Edgar may proclaim 'The gods are just' *(Act 5, Scene 3)*, but the audience is likely to think otherwise.

Ideas of justice – human and divine – permeate the play. It is natural to the human condition to want things to be 'fair' and we continue to believe this even when everything in life suggests it is not so. If the gods are indifferent to justice and human suffering, then rulers should not be. The king as the head of the state and representative of divine authority should dispense justice in a way that is seen to be fair. It is very plain in the first scene that Lear's sense of justice is subjugated to his vanity and autocratic will. The rejection of Cordelia for her honesty and Kent for his loyal plain-speaking shows a complete lack of justice, as well as blindness to the truth. It is only after much suffering that Lear acquires an insight into the way justice is meted out in his kingdom.

Lear's mock trial of Goneril and Regan shows both his madness and his new desire for justice. By the time he appears crowned with weeds in Act 4, Scene 6, he is addressing the officials responsible for carrying out justice and seeing only corruption in the beadle who lusts after the whore he has sentenced to whipping and the magistrate who, guilty himself of usury, will hang another for a lesser crime. These images of perverted justice reflect the state of Lear's mind and also the state of his kingdom.

Key quotation

Plate sin with gold,
And the strong lance of justice hurtless breaks;
Arm it in rags, a pigmy's straw does pierce it.
(Lear, Act 4, Scene 6)

Activity 3

Shakespeare's audience would have believed in a Christian religion that taught they would be judged after death on the way they behaved in life. If they repented their sins, they would be forgiven; if not, they would go to hell.

a) Discuss how far this belief can be seen in the events of the play.

- How do the characters' attitudes to justice influence their own actions?

- Is there evidence of divine justice in the play or merely of divine indifference?

b) Make notes from your discussions and keep them for revision.

Fathers and children

Lear and his daughters, Gloucester and his sons – the two families form a pattern that runs in parallel through the play. Both fathers are old and both seem unable to perceive which of their children is true and loving, and which are deceitful and unscrupulous. Both are deceived by words and neither stop to question whether they are right.

As the king, Lear has more to lose, since his actions have an impact not just on his family or followers but on the whole country. The idea of dividing a country is a metaphor for disorder and lack of harmony. To divide it between his 'pelican daughters' *(Act 3, Scene 4)*, while banishing the loving and loyal one, is a recipe for disaster. Shakespeare's audience, used to the rule of powerful monarchs, would have realized this more acutely than a modern one. The natural order that decrees children should be loyal and loving to their parents and siblings is overturned by the parents' failure to treat their children with justice and kindness.

The word 'kind' comes from the Middle English word signifying benevolent feelings like those between family members; the word can also mean members of a family or race. The meaning of 'unkind' is unnatural as well as harsh. The importance of natural feelings can be seen when Edgar guides and protects the father who cast him off and Cordelia rescues Lear and asks his blessing. When these feelings are absent, then nature itself revolts, symbolized by the storm on the heath. The elderly king, rejected by the daughters to whom he gave everything, is driven to madness, while Edmund, the natural son of Gloucester, behaves in a most unnatural fashion, plotting against his brother and then against his own father.

The natural behaviour in a family is to act for the good of everyone – just as it should be in a community or a nation. This wish is shown by Kent, Cordelia, Edgar and the Fool. It is later learned by Lear and Gloucester through hardship and suffering. Edmund, Goneril, Regan and Cornwall show no sign of behaving in any other than a purely selfish way. They have no feelings of kinship and no empathy for others. It can be argued that they have some cause – Goneril and Regan because Lear has never made any secret of the fact that Cordelia is his favourite, while Edmund, being illegitimate, will inherit nothing from his father and everything will go to Edgar. While the fathers have much to answer for, the wickedness of the children passes boundaries. No sense of morality constrains them and, as Gloucester comments to Lear, 'Our flesh and blood, my lord, is grown so vile, / That it doth hate what gets it' *(Act 3, Scene 4)*.

> **Key quotation**
>
> You lords and noble friends, know our intent;
> What comfort to this great decay may come
> Shall be appli'd
> *(Albany, Act 5, Scene 3)*

71

The children are the offspring of their fathers despite their very different behaviour and values. They can be said to represent the different aspects of their fathers.

Goneril and Regan have no compunction in their use of power, just like Lear at the start of the play. Although Lear takes himself out into the storm, they banish him from Gloucester's castle as effectively as he banishes Cordelia and Kent. Their moral blindness is a reflection of Lear's own, although carried further and with less excuse. Cordelia, on the other hand, indicates the goodness in Lear that makes him realize the suffering of others and his own moral and judicious failure.

Gloucester's adulterous nature finds an echo in Edmund, its outcome, who coolly debates which sister to take as Goneril and Regan fight over him. Gloucester's moral blindness is used against him by a natural son who is cynically aware of his own moral failings. Edgar is a product of the love and loyalty that drives Gloucester to give help to the king against the will of Goneril and Regan. Gloucester's courage in standing up to Cornwall matches Edgar's in becoming Poor Tom and protecting his father.

> **Key quotations**
>
> She that herself will sliver and disbranch
> From her material sap, perforce must wither
> And come to deadly use,
> (Albany to Goneril, Act 4, Scene 2)
>
> The gods are just, and of our pleasant vices
> Make instruments to plague us
> (Edgar to Edmund, Act 5, Scene 3)

> **Activity 4**
>
> **a)** Design a Venn diagram to show the following and how they overlap:
>
> - the public and political events
>
> - the private and domestic events.
>
> **b)** Discuss how far you agree that 'the private or familial sphere is inseparable from the public and political realm in King Lear'. Find textual evidence for your ideas.
>
> **c)** Imagine you have been asked to contribute a five-minute talk to a radio programme for students about *King Lear*. Write your talk on the integration of family and politics in the play.

Tips for assessment

You may be asked to write about themes in the exam and you should be prepared to show your knowledge of how these are presented and why Shakespeare has presented them in a particular way. For example, how and why he presents power as dynastic.

Appearance and reality, disguise and deceit

Shakespeare shows us different versions of reality in *King Lear*. The formal ceremony and ritual of the court is set against the wild nature of the heath; the pomp and rhetoric of correct manners against the raging of the storm; the gorgeous clothes and wealth of the palaces against the hardship and poverty of the wretches outside.

Many of the characters in *King Lear* are hiding their real identities for one reason or another. Some are forced to disguise their identities for fear of death, like Kent and Edgar. Others are deceitful or lying for their own ends, like Goneril, Regan and Edmund. Both Lear and Gloucester are open and honest in their dealings, although blind to the deceptions being practised upon them. Cordelia is both open and honest, and very aware of the deception used by her sisters.

Kent's loyalty brings him back from exile to serve Lear. He changes his identity from a high-born nobleman to a lowly servant by dressing roughly and adopting a local accent. He tells Lear, 'that which ordinary men are fit for, I am qualified in, and the best of me is diligence' *(Act 1, Scene 4)*. He proves his credentials by dealing with Oswald and we next see him being entrusted by Lear with messages for Regan.

Edgar's disguise, also put on from necessity, is chosen to be the biggest possible contrast to his status as heir to the earldom of Gloucester. Poor Tom, the lowest and most abject outcast, a bedlam beggar, will never be associated with the noble Edgar. Again, dramatic irony ensures the audience is taken into his confidence at intervals, telling the playgoers of Lear, 'My tears begin to take his part so much, / They mar my counterfeiting' *(Act 3, Scene 6)*. It is another irony that he tells Lear he was brought to his present state because he 'serv'd the lust of my mistress' heart, and did the act of darkness with her' *(Act 3, Scene 4)*, the fault he sees his father being punished for.

Edgar, disguised as Poor Tom, deceives his father with a masterly description of a precipice, into thinking he has survived a fall from a high cliff; 1983 TV production

Not content with playing one role, Edgar uses several others in his dealings with Gloucester. He too, uses deception, in order to persuade his father he has fallen from a high cliff and been preserved. His description of the precipice is a masterly piece of imagination that convinces Gloucester against the evidence of his other senses. As with Lear's behaviour to Kent, it is a further irony that Gloucester now trusts completely the son he cast out as a betrayer and puts his life in Edgar's hands.

Goneril and Regan appear to be dutiful and loyal daughters who put their love for their father above everything else. This is their pretence in order to pander to Lear's vanity and win a share of the kingdom. They are more successful than they hoped when Cordelia's refusal to join the rhetorical contest wins them half a realm apiece. Hardly has Lear left the stage when they are plotting how to, as the Fool puts it, 'make an obedient father' *(Act 1, Scene 4)*. Once in power their supposed love disappears, along with any vestige of filial duty or obligation. Having stripped their father of his 'additions', they shut him out from shelter in a terrible storm and it's not long before they are planning to kill him. This gross disruption of the natural order, while begun by Lear, requires minds prepared to commit both regicide and patricide. Treachery brings them together and it is fitting that they end up dying through treachery as well. Goneril poisons Regan and kills herself when her betrayal of Albany is revealed.

Edmund is an arch-deceiver. From the start of the play when he pretends to Kent, 'Sir, I shall study deserving' *(Act 1, Scene 1)*, he seems to be the dutiful son, while informing the audience of his real intentions. As with others of his villains, Shakespeare uses dramatic irony to keep the playgoers fascinated by Edmund's cleverness. He says he will take Edgar's birthright and we can only watch (and perhaps feel a sneaky admiration for) the way in which he does it. Shakespeare makes us admire his inventive mind even while we deplore the evil intentions beneath it. With the rightful heir removed, Edmund seizes the opportunity to accuse his father of treason and get himself made Earl of Gloucester prematurely. Like the sisters, he then sets out 'In pity of his misery, to dispatch / His nighted life' *(Act 4, Scene 5)*, although, also like them, his plan is thwarted.

Meanwhile, Edmund's duplicity is seen in his encouragement of both Goneril and Regan to imagine he wants them, while he debates with a breath-taking cynicism 'Which of them shall I take? / Both? one? or neither?' *(Act 5, Scene 1)* He then concludes that he will let them dispose of Albany for him, while he makes sure Lear and Cordelia are murdered. Shakespeare presents him as overreaching himself in his ambition, for all these murders would enable him to take the throne. Fittingly, his nemesis is the brother he plotted to kill.

Cordelia is the only major character in the play who practises no deception. She remains true to her own self, although it does not save her from being destroyed by evil.

Key quotation

Love well our father:
To your professed bosoms I commit him:
But yet, alas! stood I within his grace
I would prefer him to a better place.
(Cordelia, Act 1, Scene 1)

Activity 5

a) Copy and complete the table below, giving reasons and supporting evidence for the deceptions.

Character	Appearance	Reality
Kent		
Edgar		
Goneril and Regan		
Edmund		

b) There are layers of this theme for the audience to grasp. They are watching actors playing characters who themselves are pretending to be other characters. Write two or three paragraphs about Shakespeare's presentation of appearance and reality on these different levels.

Religion and belief

Shakespeare set *King Lear* in a pagan Britain where references to the gods abound. There are echoes of the classical gods Apollo, Jupiter and Juno, and of their powers. In the storm, Lear calls, 'Let the great gods, / That keep this dreadful pudder o'er our heads, / Find out their enemies now' *(Act 3, Scene 2)*. Those who have hidden crimes will believe the storm is sent to destroy them, as Jupiter was said to hurl thunderbolts at his enemies. Various characters appeal to the gods at different times. Earlier, Lear called on the goddess Nature to make Goneril sterile and in the first scene he used Hecate in a curse against Cordelia. In contrast to Lear's curse, Kent wishes 'The gods to their dear shelter take thee, maid' as he himself is banished *(Act 1, Scene 1)*. As Gloucester realizes how he misjudged his sons, even with the horror of his blinding, he asks, 'Kind gods, forgive me that, and prosper him!' *(Act 3, Scene 7)*. When Edgar pretends that Gloucester has survived his fall, he tells Gloucester, 'Think that the clearest gods, who make them honours / Of men's impossibilities, have preserved thee' *(Act 4, Scene 6)*.

Some characters see evidence of heavenly judgment in events. When Albany learns of Cornwall's death, he says, 'This shows you are above, / You justicers, that these our nether crimes / So speedily can venge!' *(Act 4, Scene 2)* When Regan and Goneril die, he calls it 'This judgment of the heavens' *(Act 5, Scene 3)*. Edgar also comments on the justice of the gods after defeating Edmund in battle. Shakespeare uses this very human desire for people to get their just deserts and sets it against the grim reality of a world where evil often wins. This is what Cordelia's death tells us and, although evil is finally overcome, the victory is hardly noticed. As Albany comments at the end of the play, 'Our present business / Is general woe' *(Act 5, Scene 3)*.

The play in Shakespeare's theatre was performed to an audience with Christian beliefs and understanding of the Bible stories. They would have seen the parallels between King Lear and Job, whose faith was tested by God in the Old Testament. They would have also been aware of Cordelia as a Christ-like figure to a limited extent. She is implicated in the repentance and redemption of her father and these two concepts are central to Christian belief. Her comment to the messenger who brings news of the British army – 'O dear father! / It is thy business that I go about' (Act 4, Scene 4) – is reminiscent of Jesus's reply to his parents when they find him in the temple. The gentleman who describes her reaction to Kent's letter about Lear's plight describes how 'she shook / The holy water from her heavenly eyes' (Act 4, Scene 3), implying something saintly about her.

The struggle between good and evil, which is a major idea in the play, was something very real to the Elizabethans, who were taught to regard heaven and hell as being in a perpetual fight for their souls. This idea is summed up in the scene where Lear awakes from his drug-induced sleep and asks Cordelia, 'You are a spirit, I know; where did you die?' (Act 4, Scene 7) He is sure he is in hell, telling her, 'I am bound / Upon a wheel of fire, that mine own tears / Do scald like molten lead' (Act 4, Scene 7). The entrance of Lear with the dead Cordelia in his arms has been likened to the famous piéta of Michelangelo, which depicts Mary holding the dead Jesus after the crucifixion. This image is a symbol for the suffering of parents, but for Christians it is viewed through belief in the Resurrection, which is notably absent in King Lear.

Motifs of punishment, suffering and reconciliation have all been seen as evidence of the play's Christian imagery. Edgar tells the defeated Edmund, 'The dark and vicious place where thee he got / Cost him his eyes' (Act 5, Scene 3), and Lear's insanity is the one thing he fears – the self-willed man losing his wits. The suffering of Lear and Gloucester leads to their ultimate reconciliation with their 'good' children.

Although Shakespeare and his audience were Christian believers, they had other ways of explaining the world around them. The idea of Fortune and her wheel

Lear carries the dead Cordelia in a way that is reminiscent of the Virgin Mary cradling the crucified Christ; Timothy West and Rachel Pickup in the 2003 Old Vic production

was popular as it gave hope to those at the bottom of society that they would go up and improve their lot. It also acted as a warning to those at the top of society that they were not immune to misfortune and could be brought low by a turn of the wheel. Lear, in his madness, says, 'I am even / The natural fool of Fortune' (Act 4, Scene 6), when he is 'captured' by Cordelia's servants. In a society where life itself was subject to outbreaks of plague and child mortality was high, it must have seemed that living a good life was not enough and that you needed a higher agency on your side.

The influence of the stars and the planets was considered important and Queen Elizabeth I had her own astrologer. When Gloucester says, 'These late eclipses in the sun and moon portend no good to us' (Act 1, Scene 2), he is only quoting the accepted viewpoint that disturbances in the natural order are a reflection of upheavals in the Chain of Being. He applies it to his own family, believing that Edgar is planning to kill him, but his reflection that 'the bond crack'd twixt son and father' is ironically close to the truth (Act 1, Scene 2).

For many people now, *King Lear* carries no hints of redemption or salvation. It is a bleak study of human cruelty and corruption that begins with hubris, continues through a wilderness of suffering and destruction, and ends without hope.

Activity 6

a) Discuss the differing philosophical views of *King Lear* and which, if any, of them you agree with:

- Christian view
- fate and Fortune
- meaningless suffering.

b) Imagine you are taking part in a debate about the presentation of belief in *King Lear*. Write a speech in which you argue your own viewpoint, supported by textual evidence.

Writing about themes

Writing about themes and motifs requires you to show knowledge and understanding of how Shakespeare presents these themes through the characters, dialogue and action. Any discussion of theme will need to analyse the language of the play, especially the recurring images. For example, if you are asked to write about the theme of power in the play, you should examine how the language used by Lear, Goneril and Regan changes in accordance with the status of the characters, as well as discussing how Shakespeare presents this changing status through actions. You will gain higher grades if you evaluate the use of, for example, animal terms for his daughters by Lear and the references to 'dotage' and weakness by the sisters.

History of *King Lear* performance

Pre-20th century

After its first performance for James I, *King Lear* became part of the repertoire. In Shakespeare's own Globe Theatre, it would have been acted with Richard Burbage as Lear and the roles of Goneril, Regan and Cordelia would have been played by boys. It has been pointed out that, since they never appear on stage together and they perform similar truth-telling functions, the actor playing Cordelia might also have been given the role of the Fool. Alternatively, the Fool could have been played by Robert Armin, the company's clown at the time. In the original Globe, it would have been performed in daylight, with minimal scenery and suitable costumes and props to indicate the different characters and their status.

The storm would have been suggested mainly by Shakespeare's words and the actors' moves and gestures, although they may have used rudimentary sound effects for the thunder and even firecrackers for the lightning strikes. Shakespeare's audience was willing to use its imagination and happy to suspend disbelief in order to enjoy dramatic events. The lack of scenery meant the action was fluid and fast paced, with one group of actors entering as another went off. Shakespeare's plays are known for their lack of stage directions, as the actors and director would have used their experience to include appropriate actions.

While audiences would have been familiar with the older version of the play, there is no record of how they reacted to Shakespeare's much bleaker version of the story. We do know that following the closing of the theatres by Oliver Cromwell after the English Civil War, the play was revived when Charles II restored the monarchy in 1660. However, the audiences of the time found it too depressing and it was rarely staged until, in 1681, the Irish poet and playwright Nahum Tate devised a new version, *The History of King Lear*, in which he rewrote the play as a love story between Edgar and Cordelia. He gave the play a happy ending in which Lear and Gloucester spent their old age being looked after by the new rulers Edgar and Cordelia.

Activity 1

Discuss what difference you think Nahum Tate's version would have made to your personal views of *King Lear*.

Theatres in the 18th and 19th centuries were mainly the property of actor-managers like David Garrick or writer-managers such as Richard Sheridan. Only two theatres were licensed for performances in London – Drury Lane and Covent Garden – so audiences were restricted in their choice until 1843, when the law was revoked and new theatres could compete. The actor-managers usually played the leading roles and chose scripts with roles in which they could star. Shakespeare was a popular choice, as he provided great characters for these stars, including King Lear.

In the 1983 TV production, Laurence Olivier played Lear against a studio set reminiscent of Stongehenge reflecting a tradition started in the 19th century

Productions in the 19th century used elaborate scenery and costumes, which meant the text had to be severely cut to allow time for lengthy scene changes. In 1838, Charles Macready decided to trust Shakespeare rather than Tate and restored the original text, including the Fool. He also set the play in Ancient Britain with scenery resembling Stonehenge, a setting that prevailed until well into the 20th century and necessitated the curtailing of scenes, like the blinding of Gloucester, to allow time for set changes. Macready also introduced rehearsals to the dramatic process. Until his innovation, the cast rarely rehearsed together with the star. The famous actor, Edmund Keane's only instruction to his fellow actors was, "stand upstage of me and do your worst."

Another great 19th-century actor, Henry Irving, managed to create an effect despite cutting 46% of the text to accommodate elaborate set changes. One audience member, Gordon Crosse, wrote of the first entrance of Lear: 'a striking figure with masses of white hair. He is leaning on a huge scabbarded sword which he raises with a wild cry in answer to the shouted greeting of his guards. His gait, his looks, his gestures, all reveal the noble, imperious mind already degenerating into senile irritability under the coming shocks of grief and age.'

Victorian sensibilities meant the scene of Gloucester's blinding was generally cut, but audiences were provided with spectacular effects of storms and battles, thanks to the invention of new stage machinery such as three-dimensional scenery, rollers which created the effect of waves on the sea, (useful for the scenes at Dover) and the moving panorama, where a long, painted cloth, unrolling as a backdrop, gave the illusion of movement. The improvements in theatre lighting, first with gaslight replacing candles, then with the use of very bright limelight and, finally, electric lighting all contributed to giving productions more realism.

> **Limelight**
>
> The saying 'in the limelight' derives from the type of very bright, white light, which was produced in theatres by heating lime. The phrase 'stealing the limelight' means drawing attention to oneself at the expense of others.

The 20th and 21st centuries

With the advent of film, *King Lear* was adapted for the screen. One of the earliest versions was a silent movie made in 1910, which was later coloured by hand. It was followed by other productions, especially after talking films became possible. Improvements in cinematography following the Second World War meant that directors could use locations and effects that were not available to the theatre.

Theatrical productions also changed as the century progressed. The last of the old-style actor-managers was Donald Wolfit, who played Lear in 1944 with the traditional Stonehenge style set, winning a glowing review from James Agate, who said it was 'the greatest piece of Shakespearean acting since I have been privileged to write for the *Sunday Times*'. The way Lear was portrayed changed from the 19th century, when he was shown as old and mentally rather frail from the start, to the mid-20th century, when actors began to play him as physically strong, as well as autocratic. This latter view meant that his decline as the play progressed was more shocking and gave more scope to the actor to show a range of skills. Views of Cordelia also changed over time, from showing her as a sweet, innocent girl to a strong woman, even a warrior as she led the French army. The Fool, too, underwent a range of interpretations from clown, to circus performer or a character from the music hall.

The brilliant and innovative director, Peter Brook, changed ideas about Lear in a radical way in his 1962 production for the Royal Shakespeare Company at Stratford. He used a huge white set, which was said by one Lear scholar to show 'both the human pathos … and the universal scale... of the scene' when Lear and Gloucester meet. The actor Paul Scofield, who played Lear, was voted the greatest ever in the role by an actors' poll at Stratford. The famous critic Kenneth Tynan (1962) wrote of the play's greatness, 'Scofield's halting, apologetic delivery of "I fear I am not in my perfect mind"; sightless Gloucester, sitting cross-legged on the empty stage while the noise of battle resounds in the wings; and the closing epiphany, wherein Lear achieves a wisdom denied him in his sanity – a Stoic determination, long in the moulding, to endure his going hence…'. It remains a ground-breaking production and, in 1971, Brook made it into a film.

Because of its universal themes, the play has been produced in many countries and in different language and theatrical traditions from Japanese Noh theatre to Indian Kathakali. Two different productions in Moscow in 1994 used it to present views of the break-up of the Soviet Union, while in Britain King Lear was first played by a female actor in a 1997 production, which was set in a crumbling nursing home where one of the patients was hallucinating. In 2016, the role was portrayed by the actress Glenda Jackson at the Old Vic to great acclaim.

In recent years, there have been many interpretations of the play, especially by the Royal Shakespeare Company and the National Theatre. In a 1993 production, directed for the RSC by Adrian Noble, the set included a floor-sized map of Britain, which Lear

Glenda Jackson played Lear, supported by Rhys Ifans as the Fool, in the Old Vic production of 2016, against backdrops with projected images to create the effects of the storm

divided with a huge marker and which thereafter disintegrated as people moved across it. It also included a rain curtain for the storm scene, which was impressive at the time. The role of Lear was taken by Robert Stephens, who was dying of cancer and whose heroic acting reduced audiences to tears.

Activity 2

a) Online, you can find the 1910 silent movie of *King Lear* and clips from the 1971 Peter Brook film. Watch both of these, making notes on the setting, costumes, actions, pacing and dramatic effects.

b) Write three paragraphs on how the views of directors about *King Lear* changed during the course of the 20th century.

Tips for assessment

You will not be expected to have a detailed knowledge of the history of the play's performance, but you will gain marks if you can show an understanding of the general ways in which it has been interpreted at different times.

Shakespeare's stagecraft

Lear is regarded as the pinnacle of an actor's career because the character is one of Shakespeare's greatest creations. The playwright's dramatic instinct, combined with the talents possessed by Richard Burbage, resulted in a character that has challenged some of our finest players, including John Gielgud, Laurence Olivier, Ian McKellen, Derek Jacobi and, more recently, Anthony Sher and Simon Russell Beale.

The opinion of Charles Lamb in 'On the Tragedies of Shakespeare' in *The Reflector* magazine, 1810–1811 that 'Lear is essentially impossible to be represented on a stage' seems to stem from his own experience of seeing 'an old man tottering about the stage with a walking stick, turned out of doors by his daughters in a rainy night'. If this is a true reflection of 18th-century performances, it's no wonder that he held this view. A.C. Bradley in *Shakespearean Tragedy* (1904) holds a similar view, for a different reason, seeing Lear as 'Shakespeare's greatest achievement, but … not his best play'. He maintains that the storm scenes have their essence in poetry, 'such poetry as cannot be transferred to the space behind the footlights, but has its being only in imagination. Here then is Shakespeare at his very greatest, but not the mere dramatist Shakespeare.'

In his *Prefaces to Shakespeare* (1946), Harley Granville-Barker refutes this idea, arguing that Shakespeare wrote *King Lear* as a play and that it shows misunderstanding to imagine that a great dramatist at the height of his powers would write an unactable play. He argues that the production values of the storm scenes do not lie in the stage effects of thunder or the use of music, but in the dialogue itself. He sees Shakespeare 'setting the actor to impersonate both Lear and – reflected in Lear – the storm'. Of the speech beginning **'Blow, winds, and crack your cheeks!'** (*Act 3, Scene 2*), he writes, 'This is no mere description of a storm, but in music and imaginative suggestion a dramatic creating of the storm itself'.

Shakespeare's use of dramatic devices in *King Lear* includes opening with a conversation between Kent and Gloucester that introduces the subplot before Lear sweeps on to the stage accompanied by his retinue. Directors in modern times have used this first scene to present their versions of Lear. He has appeared in military uniform, as commander-in-chief still, apparently able to command his forces. He has been lifted up on a throne built to look like the sun, he has entered dressed in furs and even in a wheelchair, wearing a red nose, presumably to indicate he regards the proceedings as fun. All these interpretations are justifiable in the script. Most directors show him very much the king, still in power and using it to devastating effect in his banishment of Cordelia and Kent, who hints at what is to come with his line, **'be Kent unmannerly, / When Lear is mad'** *(Act 1, Scene 1)*. This first scene holds all the clues to what will happen later in the play and is crafted so that it begins in celebration and degenerates quickly into anger and violence, as Lear draws his sword to strike at Kent. The scene ends with Goneril and Regan plotting to curb their father's rash behaviour.

For the actor playing the role, Lear presents many challenges. When asked for advice on playing Lear, the famous actor-manager Donald Wolfit is remembered for replying, 'Get a light Cordelia and keep an eye on the Fool'. For Simon Russell Beale and his director Sam Mendes, the clue to the king was violence. Lear is a violent man. In the first scene, he draws his sword on Kent and curses Cordelia, his most loved daughter. He strikes Goneril's steward, admittedly after provocation, and uses vitriolic language towards his eldest daughter. Even when mad, after his touching meeting with Gloucester, he talks of his sons-in-law and says, **'kill, kill, kill, kill, kill, kill'** *(Act 4, Scene 6)*. Finally, even when broken, he kills the man who was hanging Cordelia.

Activity 3

What advice would you give to an actor taking on the role of Lear? You might take a starting point from Lear's violence, his vanity, his moral blindness, his failings as a father or another aspect of his character.

Shakespeare moves between the main plot and the subplot, giving time for offstage action to happen. The scene between Edmund and Gloucester that establishes Edmund's unrepentant villainy begins the plot against Edgar. Shakespeare makes use of soliloquy for both Edmund and Edgar, allowing the audience into their thoughts and plans, and using dramatic irony to create suspense. When the action returns to Lear, it is to show the hostility between him and Goneril, as well as the relationship he has with the Fool, whose truth-telling he still ignores – a further source of dramatic irony, as the audience knows that the Fool is right.

An example of Shakespeare using scene juxtaposition to create effect is when he moves from Act 4, Scene 1 where Edgar finds the blinded Gloucester to Act 4, Scene 2 where Edmund is kissed by Goneril, thus emphasizing the different states of the two brothers brought about by Edmund's perfidy.

Shakespeare uses dialogue to produce dramatic effects. According to Harley Granville-Barker:

> Shakespeare's art lies in the resource which can give individual expression to a thought or emotion within the bounds, for instance, of a stretch of formal verse if his first need is for the solid strength of this; or more often in the moulding of verse and prose into such variety of expressive form that it is a wonder any unity of effect is kept at all – yet it is.
>
> (Harley Granville – Barker, *Granville – Barker's Prefaces to Shakespeare's King Lear*, 1946)

He quotes the 'seemingly haphazard mixture of verse, prose and snatches of song as we find in the scenes between Lear, Kent, Gloucester, the Fool and Poor Tom' and says 'the dramatic vitality of these scenes lies largely in this variety and balance of orchestration; their emotional strain might be intolerable without it'.

As a dramatist, Shakespeare knows what will work on stage. The confrontations between characters – Lear and Cordelia, Lear and Kent, Lear and Goneril, Kent and Oswald, Edmund and Edgar – have dramatic potential, while the blinding of Gloucester, although it can prove a headache for directors, is spellbindingly horrible.

There are scenes that are notable for their sympathy: the episode at Dover, where Edgar describes the details of the dizzying drop that Gloucester wishes to make and the touching reunion between Lear and Gloucester, one physically blind, the other blind to reason, yet both seeing more clearly. As Lear says, 'A man may see how this world goes with no eyes' *(Act 4, Scene 6)*. When Lear awakes to the presence of Cordelia and acknowledges himself 'a very foolish fond old man' *(Act 4, Scene 7)*, it is moving. Such moments give the audience respite from the suffering and fighting, although those resume shortly afterwards.

The duel between Edmund and Edgar would have been one of the highlights for Shakespeare's audience, who enjoyed a good stage fight. Modern audiences, too, like to see a well-staged battle and would feel cheated if it were not done properly. The repentance of Edmund makes the audience believe that justice will be done and the evildoers will die, while the good are saved.

Then comes Shakespeare's masterly dramatic device – the entrance of Lear, carrying the dead Cordelia and uttering the hardest line ever written for an actor, 'Howl, howl, howl!', the sound of a ruler of men reduced to an animal cry of grief *(Act 5, Scene 3)*. Lear's death seems right and merciful in the circumstances and the few who are left cannot find the right words so must 'Speak what we feel, not what we ought to say' *(Act 5, Scene 3)*.

Shakespeare used his dramatic talents to create a play that deals with the nature of humanity and its place in the universe. It is a bleak play that shows the indifference of the natural world and the evil of human beings, but also their capacity for love and the need for justice.

Lear, played by Greg Hicks, in this Royal Shakespeare Company production in 2010, with the Fool played by Kathryn Hunter

Activity 4

Imagine you have been asked to direct the first and last scenes of *King Lear*.

a) What would be your overall concept for the scenes – your interpretation of Shakespeare's text?

b) What kind of staging would you want – realistic scenery and props, a minimalist set or something in between? Describe it – design it, if you wish. Give reasons for your choices, which should relate to your overall concept.

c) How would you costume the characters to reflect their personalities – as ancient Britons, Jacobeans, in modern dress, or some other style? Describe the main characters' costumes – design them, if you wish. Give reasons for your choices, which should relate to your overall concept.

Writing about performance

In your exam, you will be expected to show knowledge of different interpretations of the play and evaluate their contribution to your understanding of the text. You will also be expected to comment on and analyse Shakespeare's dramatic methods. The wording of the question will indicate how much of your answer should be devoted to these aspects.

Critical Views

17th to 19th-century criticism

Although we have no contemporary accounts of how *King Lear* was received by its original audiences, there have been several critical views represented from later in the 17th century onwards. In Nahum Tate's preface to his own version of the play in 1681, he wrote, 'I found the whole to answer your Account of it, a Heap of Jewels, unstrung and unpolisht; yet so dazling in their Disorder, that I soon perceiv'd I had seiz'd a Treasure'. Tate's version prevailed on the stage for many years. It was approved by Samuel Johnson, in his own preface to the play, where he noted,

> In the present case the publick has decided. Cordelia, from the time of Tate, has always retired with victory and felicity. And, if my sensations could add any thing to the general suffrage, I might relate, that I was many years ago so shocked by Cordelia's death, that I know not whether I ever endured to read again the last scenes of the play till I undertook to revise them as an editor.
>
> (Samuel Johnson. *The Preface to Shakespeare*, 1765)

In the words of Arthur Murphy, a spectator to Tate's production, Lear, driven to madness by his daughters, was 'the finest tragic distress ever seen on any stage' and, in contrast, the devotion shown to Lear by Cordelia (a mix of Shakespeare's, Tate's and Garrick's contributions to the part) moved the audience to tears.

While Tate's audiences and many in the 18th century might have found Shakespeare's play too unmannerly, there were critics who didn't agree with Tate's treatment of it. In *The Spectator* on 16 April 1711, Joseph Addison wrote, '*King Lear* is an admirable Tragedy... as Shakespeare wrote it; but as it is reformed according to the chymerical Notion of poetical Justice in my humble Opinion it hath lost half its Beauty'. A century later, Charles Lamb wrote,

> Tate has put his hook in the nostrils of this Leviathan, for Garrick and his followers, the showmen of the scene, to draw the mighty beast about more easily. A happy ending! as if the living martyrdom that Lear had gone through, the flaying of his feelings alive, did not make a fair dismissal from the stage of life the only decorous thing for him. If he is to live and be happy after, if he could sustain this world's burden after, why all this pudder and preparation, why torment us with all this unnecessary sympathy? As if the childish pleasure of getting his gilt robes and sceptre again could tempt him to act over again his misused station, as if at his years, and with his experience, anything was left but to die.
>
> (Charles Lamb, 'on the Tragedies of Shakespeare,' 1811)

August Schlegel, writing at the same time, agreed with Lamb:

> I must own, I cannot conceive what ideas of art and dramatic connexion those persons have who suppose that we can at pleasure tack a double conclusion to a tragedy; a melancholy one for hard-hearted spectators, and a happy one for souls of a softer mould. After surviving so many sufferings, Lear can only die; and what more truly tragic end for him than to die from grief for the death of Cordelia? And if he is also to be saved and to pass the remainder of his days in happiness, the whole loses its signification.

(August Schlegel, *Lectures on Dramatic Art and Literature,'* 1811)

Early 19th-century critics discussed more than the problematic ending. The Romantic writers saw *King Lear* as akin to their own beliefs in the dominance of feeling over reason and the power of imagination. Samuel Taylor Coleridge wrote, of the storm scene, Act 3, Scene 4, 'what a world's convention of agonies is here! All external nature in a storm, all moral nature convulsed, – the real madness of Lear, the feigned madness of Edgar, the babbling of the Fool, the desperate fidelity of Kent – surely such a scene was never conceived before or since!'

William Hazlitt also admired the play:

> It is then the best of all Shakespeare's plays, for it is the one in which he was the most in earnest. The mind of Lear, staggering between the weight of attachment and the hurried movements of passion, is like a tall ship driven about by the winds, buffeted by the furious waves, but that still rides above the storm, having its anchor fixed in the bottom of the sea; or it is like the sharp rock circled by the eddying whirlpool that foams and beats against it, or like the solid promontory pushed from its basis by the force of an earthquake.

(William Hazlitt, *Characters of Shakespeare's Plays,'* 1817)

While, for Percy Shelley, '*King Lear,* if it can sustain this comparison, may be judged to be the most perfect specimen of the dramatic art existing in the world; in spite of the narrow conditions to which the poet was subjected by the ignorance of the philosophy of the drama which has prevailed in modern Europe'.

Tips for assessment

Depending on which exam board you are entered for, you may be asked to reference critical views in your answer. You should make sure to choose those that are relevant to the question. Even if you are not asked directly, you will gain marks by referring to critical views that support your answer.

By the end of the 19th century, after Shakespeare's original version was restored to the stage (albeit often with the text pared down), Edward Dowden gave his opinion:

> Shakespeare has dared, while paying little regard to mere historical verisimilitude, to represent the most solemn and awful mysteries of life as they actually are, without attempting to offer a ready-made explanation of them. Cordelia dies strangled in prison; yet we know that her devotion of love was not misspent. Lear expires in an agony of grief; but he has been delivered from his pride and passionate wilfulness: he has found that instead of being a master, at whose nod all things must bow, he is weak and helpless, a sport even of the wind and the rain; his ignorance of true love, and pleasure in false professions of love, have given place to an agonised clinging to the love which is real, deep, and tranquil because of its fullness. Lear is the greatest sufferer in Shakspere's plays; though so old, he has strength which makes him a subject for prolonged and vast agony; and patience is unknown to him. The elements seem to have conspired against him with his unnatural daughters; the upheaval of the moral world, and the rage of tempest in the air seem to be parts of the same gigantic convulsion.

(Edward Dowden, *Shakespeare: A Critical Study of His Mind and Art*, 1893)

For George Bernard Shaw, who spanned the 19th and 20th centuries, 'No man will ever write a better tragedy than Lear'.

Activity 1

a) Looking at the critical views on pages 86–88 from the 17th to the 19th centuries, discuss and make brief notes on the following:

- the conflict of views about the ending of the play

- Romantic views of the natural world and the pre-eminence of feeling within the play.

b) Present your ideas on the 18th-century views of the ending and the Romantic approach to the play as a talk to your class.

20th and 21st-century criticism

As Frank Kermode points out, there are many different interpretations of *King Lear* but all are partial. The Christian interpretation of Lear sees one part and the 'happy-ending' interpretation another; redemptive and the absurdist interpretations are other partial viewpoints. He argues that we should accept that we may come to know many different versions of the play, which will illuminate different aspects.

Some of the most influential critics on *King Lear* in the 20th century have interpreted the play from various angles. We can see the progression of thought from 1930 onwards, beginning with G. Wilson Knight, whose book *The Wheel of Fire* (1930) has affected much critical thinking.

Pointing out that Lear's misjudgement is 'a fault of the mind', Knight says:

> His purgatory is to be a purgatory of the mind, of madness. Lear has trained himself to think he cannot be wrong: he finds he is wrong. He has fed his heart on sentimental knowledge of his children's love: he finds their love is not sentimental. There is now a gaping dualism in his mind, thus drawn asunder by incongruities, and he endures madness. Thus the theme of the play is bodied continually into a fantastic incongruity, which is implicit in the beginning – in the very act of Lear's renunciation, retaining the title and addition of king, yet giving over a king's authority to his children. As he becomes torturingly aware of the truth, incongruity masters his mind, and fantastic madness ensues; and this peculiar fact of the Lear-theme is reflected in the 'Lear' universe.

(G. Wilson Knight, *The Wheel of Fire*, 1930)

Wilson Knight was writing about 'Lear and the comedy of the grotesque', a viewpoint picked up by Enid Welsford. She suggests:

> Like others of his profession he [the Fool] is very ready to proffer his coxcomb to his betters, but in doing so he does not merely raise a laugh or score a point, he sets a problem, 'What am I? What is madness?' he seems to ask, 'the world being what it is, do I necessarily insult a man by investing him with motley?'… It is also a central question which at once resolves itself into a question about the nature of the universe.

(Enid Welsford, *The Fool in King Lear*, 1935)

The use of a clown's mask for Rhys Ifan's Fool in the 2016 production at the Old Vic, may have reinforced questions about identity

Both of these ideas are reflected much later by Jan Kott, who applied them to the absurdist view of Lear in which he proposes the play has a form of nihilistic comedy, akin to Beckett's plays:

> The world of tragedy and the world of grotesque have a similar structure. Grotesque takes over the themes of tragedy and poses some fundamental questions. Only its answers are different… When established values have been overthrown and there is no appeal, to God, Nature or History, from the tortures inflicted by the cruel world, the clown becomes the central figure in the theatre.
>
> (Jan Kott, *Shakespeare our Contemporary*, 1963)

Writing in *Shakespearean Tragedy*, A.C. Bradley, whose comments on the ending of the play have been influential, insists that *King Lear* is defective as a play, while being great poetry. He also commented that it would have been better called 'The Redemption of King Lear', which he sees as the main thread:

> The warm castle is a room in hell, the storm-swept heath a sanctuary. The judgement of this world is a lie; its goods, which we covet, corrupt us; its ills, which break our bodies, set our souls free. Let us renounce the world, hate it, and lose it gladly. The only real thing in it is the soul, with its courage, patience, devotion. And nothing outward can touch that.
>
> (A. C. Bradley, *Shakespearean Tragedy*, 1904)

In contrast to this 'Christian' view of the play, Barbara Everett proposed a vision of the play that presents a vivid physical and imaginative recreation of experiences, but which:

> … is accompanied by something that is in one sense its diametric opposite, and in one sense an extension of itself: which is an apprehension of nothingness. There is a sense in which this apprehension of absolute cessation of being, appearing whenever the word 'nothing' drops into the dialogue, is a worse evil than any of the forms of moral evil that Lear meets.
>
> (Barbara Everett, '*The New King Lear*', 1960)

This sense of 'nothingness' is associated with the question of identity, in the view of Northrop Frye:

> … with Cordelia's 'nothing', he finds himself staring into the blankness of an empty world. Those who love Lear love him according to their bond, the tie of loyalty which is their own real life. Who is Lear to be loved apart from that? That is, what is the identity of a king who is no longer a king? Lear starts asking questions about his own identity very early, and he gets a variety of answers. 'My lady's father', says Oswald; 'Lear's shadow', says the Fool, a much shrewder person than Oswald.
>
> (Northrop Frye '*Fools of Time. Studies of Shakespearean Tragedy*', 1967)

Modern criticism has proliferated into different areas, each with their own theories and ways of interpreting the play. It is useful to examine some of these interpretations in more detail.

Feminist criticism

A feminist approach to the play looks at how male attitudes to women influence attitudes towards the female characters and the way they are presented. In the Context chapter, you looked at the patriarchal society of Shakespeare's England and how women were seen as inferior to men. It is hardly surprising to find such attitudes reproduced in plays written at that time. In fact, Shakespeare was unusual in writing roles that showed women as strong and resourceful.

A feminist view of *King Lear* considers Lear's attitudes to Goneril, Regan and Cordelia, focusing on the way his expectations of his daughters differ from Gloucester's expectations of his sons. The approach is also interested in how male attitudes towards women influence the behaviour of Lear's daughters. There are no mothers in *King Lear*, for example, so feminists consider what the effects of a lack of female role models might have on both female and male characters. How far are Goneril and Regan exhibiting male behaviour when they ruthlessly seize power when their father gives them the opportunity? Are they cruel or are they redressing the balance, asserting themselves in a world otherwise ruled by men? Feminists also focus on why Lear should curse Goneril and Regan by wishing infertility upon them and, indeed, the play contains many examples of male disgust at female sexuality.

The feminist critic Kathleen McLuskie suggests, as her central hypothesis, that the narrative and its dramatization present a connection between sexual insubordination and anarchy, and this connection suggests explicit misogyny. Therefore, the task of a feminist critic is to insist that the alternative to the patriarchal family and heterosexual love is not chaos but the possibility of new forms of social organization and affective relationships. McLuskie's method actively incorporates the assumptions of psychoanalysis as well, and mirrors the plurality and diversity of feminist criticism and political practice.

However, McLuskie also recognizes that:

> A feminist reading of the text cannot simply assert the countervailing rights of Goneril and Regan, for to do so would simply reverse the emotional structures of the play and equate feminist ideology with atavistic selfishness and the monstrous assertion of individual wills. Feminism cannot simply take "the woman's part" when that part has been so morally loaded and theatrically circumscribed.
>
> (Kathleen McLuskie, 'The Patriarchal Bard: Feminist Criticism and Shakespeare: King Lear and Measure for Measure', 1994)

For Martha Burns,

> It is all too easy to dismiss Regan and Goneril, King Lear's elder daughters, as mere emblems of female evil – the demonic opposites of their saintly younger sister, Cordelia. But Shakespeare's characters are seldom that simple […] When women are tough and ballsy, and just as obsessed with power as men, they are called evil rather than formidable. Regan and Goneril are formidable.
>
> (Martha Burns, 1996)

Kellie Bright's Regan is certainly formidable in this scene with Joseph Mydell's Gloucester, from the Globe Theatre production in 2008

S.A. Markham, in an online article about 'Lear's Girls' (2012) comments:

 … it is not simply the notion of a woman in a position of power that is problematic. Instead, the problem seems to arise when a woman is openly displaying ambition and succumbing to it with violent and, sometimes, cruel actions. These seem to be typically 'masculine' behaviours and it appears that it's the abandoning of femininity (or typically held views regarding femininity) that an audience finds both repellent and fascinating in equal measure.

(S.A. Markham, *King Lear's Girls*, 2012)

In *Re-visioning Lear's Daughters* (2010), Lesley Kordecki and Karla Koskinen write:

 Over the years, critics have written about the three overdetermined daughters, the only women in the play, stressing their part in the deterioration of their father and his kingdom through their embodiment either of evil (in the case of Goneril and Regan) or of good (in the case of Cordelia). Indeed, the frequency of the word "evil" in Lear criticism is both remarkable and lamentable. We argue that the actions of all three daughters, like those of most of the men in the play, are a result of Lear's erratic and irresponsible behaviour in the first scene. We see Lear as the flawed, at times highly sympathetic, but ultimately blind human who initiates the tragedy. These interpretations are not simple condemnatory reversals of the moral configuration of the play, but more true deconstructions of the often-assigned binaries. The older daughters are not now entirely virtuous in these readings, nor are their father and younger sister wicked. One must still feel for the magnificently articulate old man who dies at the end. But one should also feel for the women crushed in his story, despite their actions. All three are their father's daughters, led to their end by him and the environment he created. In abandoning the simplistic ethical categorizations of all the play's characters, such renderings allow the true tragedy of the story to unfold. Marvin Rosenberg does not see the daughters as "mere appendages to Lear's story" but rather says that "if they were not thought of only as Lear's daughters, the play might be their tragedy".'

(Lesley Kordecki and Karla Koskinen, *Re-Visioning Lear's Daughters*, 2010)

 Activity 3

a) Discuss the different feminist interpretations of *King Lear* given on pages 91-93, considering:

- how they might change views of Lear as a father and/or a king
- how they might change views of Goneril and Regan as '**unnatural hags**'
- how they might influence your reading of the play.

b) Write programme notes for these scenes for a new feminist production of the play.

Marxist criticism

A Marxist approach to *King Lear* would consider the play as a reflection of the political and economic structures of the society in which it was written. It would view Lear as a feudal lord only interested in personal power, who has exploitative relationships with his subjects or neglects them and their welfare. This approach looks particularly at Lear's realization in Act 3, Scene 4 that he has taken 'Too little care' of the 'Poor naked wretches' in his kingdom. It would also focus on reading the instances of commercial-style bargaining in the love competition to see who gets the biggest share of land, in what Cordelia is worth in terms of her dowry and in Lear's assessment of his daughters' worthiness by the number of possessions or knights he can keep after his abdication.

> **Marxism**
>
> Marxism describes the political and economic theories of Friedrich Engels and Karl Marx, the 19th-century economist and philosopher who wrote *Das Kapital*, a critique of capitalism, and *The Communist Manifesto*.

Marxism is founded on class structures, economic power and the possible re-distribution of wealth in an ideal world. Insofar as Lear is a privileged ruler, he is deprived of understanding; insofar as he gains knowledge, he is incapable of ruling and ashamed of privilege. This has a modern ring in that governments (in this case, the king) remain ignorant of the conditions faced by the poor and so their legislation is aimed at the wealthy and powerful, thus ensuring that inequality continues. In order for Lear to discover the true condition faced by most of his subjects, he has to become an outcast, depending, like them, on the whims of those in power. When he realizes the injustice and corruption taking place, it's too late for him to change things. As Davide Walsh says on the World Socialist website (2002):

> The family and social dilemmas come together in this. The normal ruler is trained to shut his eyes to the misery of the population. Lear becomes vulnerable to a wider reality when he puts himself at the mercy of his daughters and finds himself suddenly homeless and stripped of his retinue and privileges. He discovers a far greater tragedy than his own in the condition of those with whom he shares the open heath in Act 1, Scene 2. At this point the family tragedy turns into something else.

Activity 4

One of Marx's famous quotations is, 'From each according to his means; to each according to his needs'. What references can you find in *King Lear* that might lead to a similar idea?

Kiernan Ryan writes in 'Sovereignty Subversion in *King Lear*' (2016) that 'No account of *King Lear* that fails to face the conflict it dramatises between the inhuman drive to divide and dominate epitomized by a king, and the human need for equality, kindness and community embodied by a naked beggar, can begin to do justice to the tragedy Shelley called 'the most perfect specimen of the dramatic art existing in the world'. Through the harrowing transformations of Lear, Gloucester and Edgar the play demolishes the pillars of disparity that support all forms of class society, then and now, and the unequal distribution of wealth and power on which class society depends. It climaxes in Lear's snarl of contempt for all who claim the right to impose their will on others: 'a dog's obey'd in office' (Act 4, Scene 6). And in place of institutionalised greed, exploitation and oppression the tragedy advocates a compassionate, egalitarian ethic, rooted in the fundamental kinship of all human creatures: 'So distribution should undo excess, / And each man have enough'.

In *Shakespeare: A Marxist Interpretation* (1936), the Soviet critic Aleksandr A. Smirnov wrote of Lear that, 'Having endured need and privation, he begins to understand a great deal of what had hitherto been incomprehensible, and to regard his power, his life, and mankind in a different light.'

In the deepest sense, however, *King Lear* is far more than the tragedy of an individual or group of individuals. In *Literature and Revolution* (1924), Leon Trotsky suggested, the individual passion is carried to such a high degree of tension that it outgrows the individual, becomes super-personal, and is transformed into a fate of a certain kind.

Marxism also rejects the idea of primogeniture (the right of the eldest legitimate son to inherit title and land from his father) as inherently unfair. Paul W. Kahn points out:

> Edmund is the most dangerous and treacherous of the characters. Yet, he begins from a cause that we cannot identify as unjust. By placing himself ahead of his brother, he is only rejecting the fate that law had dealt him. If there is no justice in Edmund's plan, neither was there any justice in Edgar's legal entitlement.

(Paul W. Kahn, *Law and Love: The Trials of King Lear*, 2000)

Evolutionary approach

In *An Evolutionary Approach to Shakespeare's King Lear*, Joseph Carroll argues:

> From an evolutionary perspective, if people wish to justify ethical values they can look for justification only within a purely human context. Edgar's comment to Gloucester "Men must endure / Their going hence even as their coming hither; / The ripeness is all" fulfils this evolutionary idea.

(Joseph Carroll, *An Evolutionary Approach to Shakespeare's King Lear*, 2013)

The Marxists identify economic class as the chief constituent in social relations. That preconception blocks insight into *King Lear* in two important ways: it gives no adequate access into the feelings of reverence associated with Renaissance conceptions of royalty and it obscures the sense of a common humanity.

Evolutionary critics agree that language has a function in communicating information and shared experience, which is what Shakespeare is doing in *King Lear* by creating emotional and imaginative links between dramatist and audience. He can rely on the audience despising hypocrisy and abuse of power, and their willingness to be guided by characters such as Kent and Cordelia in their responses to Lear and others.

Activity 5

a) Discuss the different approaches of Marxist and evolutionary critics. Work with a partner, if possible, or on your own to do the following:

- Summarize each approach in bullet points, drawing on the statements on pages 94-96.

- Find quotations from the play that could be used to justify each approach.

- Give your own views on how each of these approaches has illuminated the play (or not).

b) Write two paragraphs on how you imagine a production of *King Lear* directed according to each interpretation might look.

Psychoanalytical approach

The psychoanalytic critical approach is heavily influenced by the writings of Sigmund Freud. The approach focuses on characters' motivations, in particular investigating 'hidden' desires, fears, etc., which may be in conflict with explicitly acknowledged feelings. In her novel *A Thousand Acres*, a modern reworking of *King Lear*'s story, Jane Smiley portrays the Lear character as an incestuous tyrant. Such an approach to *King Lear* bears fruit when it considers how living with an unreasonably demanding father may affect his children's attitudes and states of mind. It might also consider the effect of the absence of a mother in both the Lear story and the Gloucester subplot, as well as the psychological effect of Edmund being born out of wedlock.

For Coppelia Kahn:

The play's beginning is marked by the omnipotent presence of the father and the absence of the mother. Yet in Lear's scheme for parcelling out his kingdom, we can discern a child's image of being mothered. He wants two mutually exclusive things at once: to have absolute control over those closest to him and to be absolutely dependent on them.

(Coppelia Kahn, 'The Absent Mother in King Lear', 2012)

Philip D. Collington argues:

 King Lear depicts various nefarious effects of public life and companionship on the individual self [...] What is at issue is not Lear's 'dependency behaviour': no one in the play disputes his legitimate need for assistance because of advancing age or his royal prerogative for assistants even after he has divested his authority. Instead, what is at issue is Lear's choice of companions, the number of companions, the activities encouraged by his companions, and most importantly, their moral fitness to accompany the king.

(Philip D. Collington 'Self-discovery in Montaigne's "Of Solitarinesse" and King Lear', 2002)

A Freudian reading of the play, as suggested by Magdalena Stawicka, sees Lear having a 'mother-fixation' on his daughters, which leads him to demand their undivided love and attention. She suggests that such an interpretation would show his elder daughters as intuiting his need when they make their protestations of love, and would also account for his unreasonable rage and rejection of Cordelia for refusing it, and his terrible curse on Goneril for what he might unconsciously view as castration, in demanding a diminution of his train.

Activity 6

a) Summarize briefly what you understand to be the position of the psychoanalytical approach.

b) Write brief answers to the following:

- What does this view have to offer in terms of interpreting the play?
- What would you take from this approach to help with your own writing about *King Lear* and why?

Writing about critical views

While you will be expected to know the main critical views that have been used in interpreting the play, both in scholarship and performance, it will not form a major part of any exam question. If you wish to gain the highest grades, you should show familiarity with the most important critics pre-20th century, and with the various modern approaches that have proliferated in the 20th and 21st centuries.

The exam

The exam questions are designed to test:

- your knowledge and understanding of the play
- your ability to perceive the writer's intentions
- your ability to comment on and analyse the play's relationship to its genre and context
- your approach to the play as a performance
- how you select and evaluate different interpretations of the play.

You will also be judged on your:

- writing ability
- use of appropriate technical vocabulary
- use of well-chosen references and suitable integrated quotations to support your ideas
- ability to construct an argument.

It is very demanding to write an exam essay on such a complex play so organizing your time and careful planning are essential (see the section on planning on page 101).

Understanding the question

You may be given an extract from the play and be asked to comment on it, either by a close reading of aspects of the text or relating it to the play as a whole, or both. You may be given a straightforward essay-style question, often based on a quotation from a critic. You may have to answer both types of question or, alternatively, choose one or the other. It will depend which exam board you are entered with. If you are given an extract, you should use it to comment in detail on features of Shakespeare's language and imagery, as well as relating it to themes and characters. You may also be asked specifically to comment on context, genre, different interpretations (critical views) or dramatic methods. Even if you are not directly requested to do so, you should try to show some knowledge of these areas in your answer. You will not be expected to identify any critical quotations, but you should use them to guide your argument (either for or against).

You should approach the question in an efficient way by identifying what you are being asked to do. That means underlining or highlighting the key words and phrases, and noting what they mean. Sometimes it helps to write them in your own words. This is an important stage as many students lose marks in exams because they fail to answer the actual question. Examiners often use particular words and phrases, which you can learn to interpret and that should guide the way you shape your answers.

Explore: This well-used word means you will be expected to look at the different aspects of the topic. For example, 'Explore Shakespeare's presentation of family relationships' means you should look at how the two families in the play are presented, both in literary and dramatic terms; the connections between family and constitutional power; the 'good' children and the 'bad' children; and differences and problems between the generations. You will also need to show how they fit into the genre of tragedy; how they are seen in the context of Shakespeare's England; and how different critical views would interpret them.

Examine: Similar to 'explore', this means using much the same techniques in your answer.

Consider: This word is often accompanied by a particular view – or perhaps quotation – and expects you to construct an argument either agreeing or disagreeing with it. In either case you will need to analyse the given viewpoint and show clearly that you understand what it means and why it is held, before going on to expand your own views and ideas. These must be thoughtfully stated, well supported by evaluation of textual references, and related to critical interpretations, contextual points and the play in performance. One example might be, 'Consider the view that the question "What is a man?" lies at the centre of *King Lear*'. You may want to agree that the core of the play is about what it means to be human or you may want to disagree and argue that it is about something else. Either way, you should discuss why the view is a valid one, before going on to give your own opinions.

To what extent: This phrase is usually asking you about a statement preceding the question, such as '"The theme of *King Lear* is the decay and fall of the world." (Jan Kott) How far do you agree with this view?' As with a 'consider' question, you should evaluate the validity of the view before arguing for or against it. In this case, it might help if you know that Jan Kott is a critic who sees *King Lear* as an absurdist text and has compared it with the plays of Samuel Beckett, as well as influencing Peter Brooke's production. You may decide that this view is one you share and that its extent covers everything in the play. You may disagree with it and see it as too encompassing, or you may see it as one of several themes or not the dominant one. Again, you should examine the validity of the statement before expanding your own ideas.

How far do you agree: This is a similar phrase to 'To what extent' and should be treated in the same way.

Show how: This is an invitation to write about Shakespeare's techniques as a writer, poet and dramatist. For example, 'Show how the subplot in *King Lear* complements the story of Lear himself.' You will need to write about how Shakespeare presents the two old men, both as fathers and as members of the ruling elite. This will involve showing that their fates are similar but different; how their journeys, physical and spiritual, are parallel but also divergent; and how these similarities and differences reinforce the themes and ideas of the play. Your knowledge of performance values and critical views will be especially useful here as you can show how Shakespeare's stagecraft and ideas have been interpreted by directors and scholars.

Look at the question below. The key words and phrases have been explained.

Look at all the aspects.

The characters most responsible

Explore the idea that Edgar and Cordelia are the main upholders of moral values in *King Lear*.

Doing the right thing and staying uncorrupted

You can see that you are being asked to do several things here. You should write about:

- whether Edgar and Cordelia do in fact uphold moral values and how this is shown
- whether they do remain uncorrupted and what evidence there is of this
- whether there are other characters in the play who might have a claim to be considered (Kent, the Fool, Albany)
- how these moral values are decided in the play and what they are contrasted with
- different interpretations of the moral role played by the two characters.

Activity 1

Look at the question below.

> Consider the view that *King Lear* is ultimately a play about love and forgiveness.

a) Highlight or underline the key words and phrases. Then describe what you are being asked to do.

b) Make a bullet point list of references and examples (and perhaps short quotations) you need in order to answer the question.

c) Make a brief list of any relevant performance and critical interpretations you might refer to.

d) Jot down any points relating to context or genre that could be helpful.

Activity 2

Imagine you are a chief examiner.

a) Write two or three questions you think would test the assessment objectives for this part of the exam. (The assessment objectives can be found on the website of your exam board.)

b) Swap with another student and analyse each other's questions as in Activity 1.

Tips for assessment

To gain the higher grades in the exam you need to show that you have thought about the play for yourself and can give your own opinions about what Shakespeare is saying and how he is saying it, supporting your views with well-chosen references and quotations. You will also need to show that you have considered the text as a tragedy and as a play to be performed, and that you are able to judge relevant critical interpretations.

Planning your answer

With so many areas to consider, it is well worth taking a few minutes to plan your answer. That way you have all the outline information you need and can concentrate on your writing style and correct use of terminology. Once you have analysed the question and understand what you need to include, you can plan your answer.

Examiners always make the point that candidates who use their own ideas about the text produce fresher and more interesting answers than candidates who have prepared essays in advance. So the key is to practise planning answers to a variety of questions and, if you do want to write full answers for practice, do not try to learn them by heart. It is unlikely that they will match the exact question you are asked and you risk being irrelevant.

Extract-based questions

When you are answering a question on an extract from the text, like the one below, you will be expected to do some close reading and show that you understand Shakespeare's use of literary techniques.

> Read the section in Act 3, Scene 2 from Kent's entrance, 'Lear: No, I will be the pattern of all patience…' to' Lear: … That's sorry yet for thee.'
>
> With close reference to the language and imagery in this passage, examine how Shakespeare presents the changes taking place in Lear out on the heath.

The most useful thing about a plan is that you can jot down all the ideas that come into your head as you read and then concentrate on structuring your answer. Use the question as your starting point and, having analysed what you are required to do, write down the main points of your answer as bullet points or as a spider diagram, depending on which method works for you.

You could make brief bulleted notes about the question on page 101 like this:

1) Changes in Lear
- Lear talks of patience – something he usually lacks
- He says the gods are finding out hidden criminals – not him
- He ignores Kent, but pities the Fool – unusual
- Shows him thinking about others
- Shows him talking about justice – main theme
- Contrast between castle and hovel – one rich and 'cold', one poor and 'warm'

2) Language and imagery
- Kent sees 'gallows', 'dark', 'sheets of fire', 'bursts', 'groans', too much for humans (hostility of nature)
- Lear talks of 'wretches', 'undivulged crimes', 'unwhipp'd of Justice', 'perjur'd', 'simular man of virtue', 'incestuous,' 'caitiff... practis'd on man's life', 'close pent-up guilts' and contrasts with 'man more sinn'd against than sinning'. (He is not a hypocrite.)
- Kent talks of 'hovel' (ironic contrast with castle), 'hard house' (not physical), 'Denied me to come in', 'scanted courtesy' (hostility of people)
- Lear refrain 'my wits begin to turn'. Care for Fool shown in 'How dost my boy?', 'Art Cold?', 'Poor Fool and knave', 'one part in my heart that's sorry'
- Change of lifestyle – and mind – 'art of our necessities is strange, / And can make vile things precious'.

A spider diagram on the same question might look like the example opposite. These diagrams can be useful if you want to add more connecting ideas as you think of them.

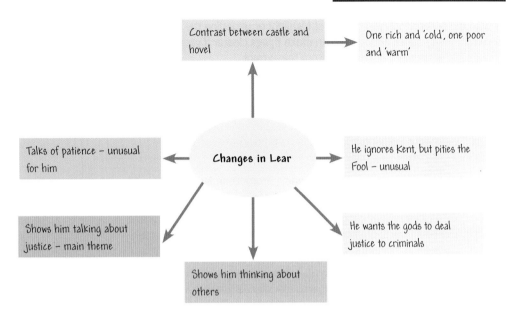

Contrast between castle and hovel → One rich and 'cold', one poor and 'warm'

Talks of patience – unusual for him ← **Changes in Lear**

He ignores Kent, but pities the Fool – unusual

Shows him talking about justice – main theme

He wants the gods to deal justice to criminals

Shows him thinking about others

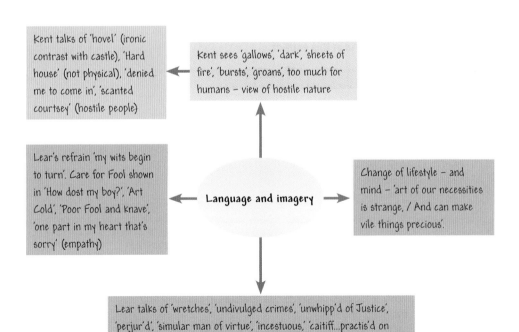

Kent talks of 'hovel' (ironic contrast with castle), 'Hard house' (not physical), 'denied me to come in', 'scanted courtsey' (hostile people) ← Kent sees 'gallows', 'dark', 'sheets of fire', 'bursts', 'groans', too much for humans – view of hostile nature

Lear's refrain 'my wits begin to turn'. Care for Fool shown in 'How dost my boy?', 'Art Cold', 'Poor Fool and knave', 'one part in my heart that's sorry' (empathy) ← **Language and imagery** → Change of lifestyle – and mind – 'art of our necessities is strange, / And can make vile things precious'.

Lear talks of 'wretches', 'undivulged crimes', 'unwhipp'd of Justice', 'perjur'd', 'simular man of virtue', 'incestuous', 'caitiff...practis'd on man's life', 'close pent-up guilts' and contrasts with 'man more sinned against than sinning'. (He is not a hypocrite.)

As with the bulleted list, you could just highlight or underline the textual quotations you want on the paper, although it can make things clearer if you select words and phrases and write them down away from the extract.

Activity 3

a) If possible, work with a partner or in small group, and each take one of the following questions. Use either a spider diagram or a bullet list to plan an answer to your question.

1

> Look at the extract in Act 1, Scene 1, from 'Lear: Now, our joy...' to 'Lear: ... As thou my sometime daughter.'
>
> With close reference to the language and imagery in this passage, examine how Shakespeare presents the characters of Lear and Cordelia in this extract.

2

> Look at the extract in Act 1, Scene 2, from 'Gloucester: These late eclipses...' to 'Edmund: .... *Fa, sol la mi.*'
>
> With close reference to the language and imagery in this passage, examine how Shakespeare presents the relationship between Gloucester and Edmund in this extract.

3

> Look at the extract in Act 4, Scene 2, from 'Goneril: I have been worth the whistle' to 'Goneril: ... Marry, your manhood – mew!'
>
> With close reference to the language and imagery in this passage, examine how Shakespeare presents the marriage of Goneril and Albany in this extract.

4

> Look at the extract in Act 5, Scene 3, from 'Edmund: What you have charg'd me with...' to 'Edmund: ... something more to say.'
>
> With close reference to the language and imagery in this passage, examine how Shakespeare presents the changes in Edmund and Edgar from the start of the play.

b) Share and discuss your plan with the rest of the group and amend it if you wish.

Tips for assessment

Don't spend too long on your plan – 5 minutes should be adequate – or you may run out of time to complete your answer.

Don't cross out your plan because if you do run out of time, it will be taken into consideration. Examiners are not allowed to mark work that has been crossed out.

Remember, if you are answering a question based on a printed extract from the play, you will need to identify, comment on and evaluate the language features and imagery. To gain the higher grades, you will need to relate these to the specific question being asked, and show how Shakespeare's use of language and imagery are essential to the audience's understanding of the characters and themes in the play. For example, in Edmund's first soliloquy (Act 1, Scene 2), you would need to show:

- how Shakespeare's use of the soliloquy format and blank verse contribute to our first impressions of Edmund
- how the repetition of words such as 'legitimate' and 'bastard' reveal his feelings about his status
- how the use of imagery involving 'nature' raises questions about justice
- how Shakespeare uses dramatic irony to allow him to manipulate the audience, as well as his father and brother.

Writing your answer

When you have your plan, know roughly what you want to say and how you will approach the question, you need to consider how to structure your answer. What you are aiming for is a thoughtful and coherent argument of your views, based on textual evidence and different interpretations. Look at the question below:

> Consider the view that *King Lear* is ultimately a play about love and forgiveness.

- Your introduction might outline the views of love shown in *King Lear*, e.g. conditional love, as linked to the commercial value of dowries or numbers of retainers; unconditional and spontaneous love, as shown by Cordelia to Lear, France to Cordelia and Edgar to Gloucester; love linked to loyalty, as with Kent and the Fool. A second paragraph might briefly show how forgiveness is linked to love and how it is shown by each of these characters.

- Your development would look in more detail at how these views of love and forgiveness might be linked to Christian virtues by Shakespeare's audience (context), to a more detailed evaluation of how this love and forgiveness is shown in the play (reference performance) and the grief caused by the loss of loved ones after reconciliation (reference critical views on the ending).

- Your conclusion could argue whether Shakespeare's presentation of love and forgiveness represents the 'ultimate' theme and idea of the play, or whether it should be regarded as equal to or less than other themes such as suffering, power or justice.

You need to pay close attention to the quality of your writing in your answer. You should use literary terms appropriately and with confidence, show familiarity with alternative views and with Shakespeare's dramatic method, and be able to support your ideas with well-chosen textual references, including short quotations.

There are degrees of response that may determine which grade you achieve.

- At a basic level, you will need to show a general understanding of the text and the way in which it is written; attempt to engage with the details of the text and how it shapes meaning; demonstrate some notion of the influence of context and genre, and their significance; show awareness of different interpretations; and give simple, generalized organization to your argument.

- At a higher level, you will give clear, logical structure to your argument; engage with relevant areas of the text; select relevant textual references and show how they shape meaning; show how contextual factors influence genre; confidently use critical terminology and show awareness of different interpretations and their connection to your own views; and discuss the play in performance.

- At the highest level, you will demonstrate a sophisticated awareness of the way the writer works both as author and playwright in performance; create a critical evaluative argument, well supported by textual reference; show confident use of alternative readings to illuminate your own argument and perceptive understanding of the significance of contextual factors in relation to the text.

Using textual references and quotations

It is most important that you can demonstrate the evidence on which your opinions are based. Few marks, if any, will be awarded if you state, e.g. 'King Lear brings all his troubles on himself when he divides his kingdom', without showing why you think this. Your assertion would need to be supported by references to how Lear behaves to Kent and Cordelia, the way Goneril and Regan behave to Lear, and what this leads to when he is shut out on the heath. Each reference should be supported, in turn, by a short, relevant quotation where possible.

A simple rule is that every statement you make or idea you propose should be backed up by evidence. One way to ensure this is to ask yourself: 'How do I know this?' or 'Why do I think this?' The answer should provide the evidence.

It is obviously easier to comment in detail about language and imagery when you are given an extract from the play. However, examiners in closed-book exams will accept more general quotations, so it is a good idea to learn a selection of quotations appropriate to different themes and characters. For example, Gloucester's lines, 'As flies to wanton boys, are we to th'gods; / They kill us for their sport' *(Act 4, Scene 1)*, could be used in questions about the use of the subplot; the characters of Gloucester and of Edgar; the themes of suffering, power and justice; the tragic genre, the religious context and theatre of the absurd.

At a basic level you might use this quotation in support of an opinion, perhaps about Edgar's wish to protect his father from suicide. At a higher level you might evaluate this anti-religious sentiment in terms of Edgar's somewhat rigid moral code and the contextual influence of Shakespeare's Christian audience, for whom suicide meant going to hell.

When using quotations, it is best to keep them short and integrate them into your argument. For example, you might write, 'Lear's concern is for his sanity as he mentions it several times, telling the Fool, "let me not be mad" some time before he actually loses his reason.' In this way you make your evidence an integral part of your argument.

If you should need a longer quotation or if, for example, you wanted to make a point about Shakespeare's use of blank verse, you would need to mark this off from the main body of your text. For example:

> When Shakespeare presents Lear as defying the elements, he uses the verse drama form to emphasize the universal nature of the feelings:
>
> 'Blow, winds, and crack your cheeks! rage! blow!
> You cataracts and hurricanoes, spout
> Till you have drench'd our steeples, drown'd the cocks!'

You would then continue by evaluating the quotation in the context of the question and the wider themes and imagery of the play.

Tips for assessment

Remember that while you need to show your knowledge and understanding of plot, structure, context, characters, language, genre, themes, performance and critical views, these must *always* be relevant to the task you have been set. This means you need to be selective in the information you use and never just write about any of them unless they illustrate your argument.

Sample questions

1

Explore the significance of this extract from Act 4, Scene 6, from 'Gloucester: When shall I come to th'top of that same hill?' to 'Gloucester: ... Now, fellow, fare thee well', with regard to the tragedy of the whole play. You should remember to analyse Shakespeare's dramatic methods.

2

'The death of Cordelia [...] has only pain to make it meaningful.' To what extent do you agree with this view? You should include relevant comments on Shakespeare's dramatic methods.

3

This question is in **two parts**. In **both part (i)** and **part (ii)** you are required to analyse how meanings are shaped.

In **part (ii)** you are **also** required to:

- Show wider knowledge and understanding of the play you have studied

- Take account of relevant contexts and different interpretations which have informed your reading.

Read the extract from Act 2, Scene 4, from 'Goneril: Why might not you, my lord...' to 'Lear: ... O Fool! I shall go mad'.

(i) With close reference to the language and imagery in this passage, examine how Shakespeare presents power within family relationships.

(ii) Consider the view that Shakespeare's presentation of family and political disunity has universal significance.

4

Explore Shakespeare's presentation of justice and corruption in *King Lear*. You must relate your discussion to relevant contextual factors and ideas from your critical reading.

5

Explore the significance of this extract from Act 4, Scene 6, from 'Gloucester: O, let me kiss that hand!' to 'Lear: ... To see the things thou dost not', with regard to the tragedy of the whole play. You should remember to analyse Shakespeare's dramatic methods.

6

'Lear's two monstrous daughters, Goneril and Regan, are archetypal villains from the onset of the play.' How far do you agree with this assessment? You should include relevant comments on Shakespeare's dramatic methods.

7

This question is in **two parts**. In **both part (i)** and **part (ii)** you are required to analyse how meanings are shaped.

In **part (ii)** you are **also** required to:

- Show wider knowledge and understanding of the play you have studied
- Take account of relevant contexts and different interpretations which have informed your reading.

Read the extract from Act 4, Scene 7, from 'Cordelia: How does my royal lord?' to 'Lear: I am old and foolish'.

(i) With close reference to the language and imagery in this passage, examine how Shakespeare presents the reconciliation between Lear and Cordelia.

(ii) Examine the view that *King Lear* uses poverty and the notion of suffering to present the concept of Christian redemption.

8

Explore Shakespeare's presentation of blindness and perception in *King Lear*. You must relate your discussion to relevant contextual factors and ideas from your critical reading.

 Activity 4

a) Choose one of the sample questions on page 108 or 109 and practise your response as follows:

- plan your answer using either a bullet list or a spider diagram
- write an outline of your answer, including an introduction, development and a conclusion
- make a list of relevant textual references to support your views
- find appropriate quotations as evidence
- make a list of relevant contextual factors
- note points of dramatic method related to genre
- jot down any suitable critical views either for or against your argument.

b) Write your answer against the clock, giving yourself approximately one hour.

Sample answers

Sample answer 1

This question is in **two parts**. In **both part (i)** and **part (ii)** you are required to analyse how meanings are shaped.

In **part (ii)** you are **also** required to:

- Show wider knowledge and understanding of the play you have studied
- Take account of relevant contexts and different interpretations which have informed your reading.

Read the extract from Act 2, Scene 4, from 'Goneril: Why might not you, my lord…' to 'Lear: … O Fool! I shall go mad'.

(i) With close reference to the language and imagery in this passage, examine how Shakespeare presents power within family relationships.

(ii) Consider the view that Shakespeare's presentation of family and political disunity has universal significance.

Part (i)

In this extract the audience sees how power has shifted from Lear to Goneril and Regan. Having quarrelled with Goneril, Lear went to Regan, only to find that she is at Gloucester's castle, where he has followed her. Lear has just realized that the two sisters are joined against him. Goneril asks, quite reasonably, why Lear couldn't be attended by 'those that she calls servants, or from mine?' The two women speak politely to their father, addressing him as 'my lord' and making a case that is logical. If their servants 'chanc'd to slack ye / We could control them', Regan points out, contrasting with Goneril's accusations of rowdy behaviour among Lear's knights. With implacable courtesy, they bargain the number down to 'five-and-twenty'. Lear, measuring love in terms of retainers, forgets his dreadful curse on Goneril for wanting to reduce him to fifty and says 'thou art twice her love'. Goneril promptly shows her power by mentioning 'five-and-twenty, ten, or five' and is topped by Regan with 'What need one?' This language is like a reverse auction and recalls the 'which of you loves me most' competition in return for land at the start of the play.

Gives a clear statement of the premise.

Good use of embedded quotations.

Thoughtful point relates the extract to the whole play.

Perceptive analysis of language in the extract and elsewhere in the play.

Accurate point about the use of blank verse.

Evaluates imagery and language.

Quotation well selected to illustrate meaning.

Shakespeare uses blank verse to show the formal nature of the exchanges and the language of commerce to reveal the balance of power in which the two sisters hold all the cards. Without the 'additions' of his authority – land and men – Lear can only rage 'O, reason not the need!', as he argues that if men have nothing more than 'needs' then human 'life is cheap as beast's'. He uses the image of 'basest beggars' and contrasts this with 'what thou gorgeous wear'st' – the fine clothes that barely do their job of providing warmth. He appeals to the gods to give him patience, but then to 'touch me with noble anger' so he won't cry. It is ironic that he

Makes indirect reference to feminist theory in context of play.

refers to tears as 'women's weapons' since he is the only one shedding them while the sisters remain adamant. The patience for which he asked is little in evidence as he swears revenge on 'you unnatural hags', although his realization that he has no means of carrying this out reduces him to

Thoughtfully compares language and state of mind with the brewing storm.

incoherence. His broken sentences and phrases, such as 'terrors of the earth', which mean nothing are set against the ominous and real terror of the coming storm, when Lear defiantly refuses to weep but is fearful: 'O Fool! I shall go mad'. The repetition of 'tears' and 'weep' reinforces his

Well-made point shows close reading.

passion, while his reference to madness, a recurrent fear, prophesizes what will happen to him out on the heath.

Part (ii)

This scene is the culmination of a family breakdown that is also a political breakdown, stemming from the division of the kingdom, which is rapidly becoming division within the kingdom. The feudal nature of Lear's society

Gives relevant contextual comment.

means that the crown passes through a dynastic succession and, without sons, Lear's daughters naturally inherit. Shakespeare's audience, used to an absolute monarchy, would have understood this. Lear's intention

Makes an insightful point about the family/power balance.

was to prevent quarrels over the succession by parcelling out the land before his death. His vanity and autocratic nature led him to devise a contest in which hypocritical rhetoric was preferred to sincerity. Thus, to the blindness of his decision to give up his kingdom while imagining he could keep the respect due to a monarch, was added the loss of the one daughter who might have made it work.

Feminist theory sees the three daughters as victims of Lear's folly just as much as he is a victim of his own passions and, later, of the elements. Goneril and Regan can be seen as monsters – especially as the play continues. However, they are not merely symbols of evil but the children of a man who loses his identity when he abdicates. Lear has defined himself through his role as king more than as father – witness his rage when his question to Oswald is answered with 'You are my lady's father'. When he no longer holds the position of king, as Northrop Frye has pointed out, he becomes, in the Fool's words, 'Lear's shadow'.

Makes a perceptive reference to feminist theory.

Offers a thoughtful idea, well supported by critical reference and textual evidence.

Generally this is a thoughtful approach to the question, which shows understanding of Shakespeare's meanings and techniques. The candidate attempts to answer the question and shows perceptive arguments well supported by textual and critical references. The answer could have been improved by a more detailed exploration of the universal significance of the disunity in the play and dwells too much on the family power struggles, although these are clearly evaluated.

Sample answer 2

'The death of Cordelia has only pain to make it meaningful.' To what extent do you agree with this view? You should include relevant comments on Shakespeare's dramatic methods.

Sets out a clear premise about the ending of the play and different views.

People have argued about the ending of *King Lear* for more than 300 years. Some critics thought the play was unactable and Nahum Tate changed the ending to make it happier, with Lear and Gloucester retiring and Cordelia marrying Edgar and living happily ever after. Why does Shakespeare have Cordelia die? After all the suffering Lear has gone through, it just seems more cruelty to lose his favourite daughter just when he has found her again.

Makes a somewhat basic assertion about the 'love contest' but shows understanding.

Makes a clear statement of cause and effect, although rather baldly stated.

In the first scene of the play when Lear holds a competition to see which of his daughters loves him most, Goneril and Regan make flowery speeches about how much they love their father. Lear believes them, although Cordelia knows they are faking. When it is her turn, all she says is 'Nothing'. This is because she really loves him as a daughter, but she won't say things she doesn't feel. Unfortunately, Lear takes words at face value and doesn't see true feelings. When he banishes Cordelia, he starts the train of events that lead to her death. This is because he allows Goneril and Regan to have half the kingdom each and this leads to the country being torn apart and to evil getting the upper hand. This evil, working through Goneril, Regan and Edmund, is responsible for all the suffering and death that follows.

Shows awareness of dramatic methods and how they work although in an unsophisticated way.

In the first scene, Shakespeare uses some dramatic moments, like when Lear curses Cordelia and casts her off as his child, and when Kent defies him and Lear tries to kill him with his sword, and has to be restrained. These moments help to show the audience that Lear is an angry and violent man, who is ruled by passion rather than reason. He only learns to be a good person, not just a king, by suffering madness and rejection. It is Cordelia who rescues him, helped by Kent. The two people he treated unjustly show him love and forgiveness and save him after he loses his wits.

Perceptive comment on the roles of Kent and Cordelia needs development.

The first we hear of Cordelia after she goes to France is when Kent reads her letter and we know they have kept in touch. Later, after Lear arrives in Dover, we hear from Kent that Lear is now too ashamed to meet his youngest daughter but that she has wept to hear about his sufferings. When they finally meet again, Lear thinks Cordelia is 'a soul in bliss' while he is in hell. After they are reconciled, he confesses he is 'a very foolish fond old man' and no longer sees himself as a king but as a father. This makes Cordelia rather like a Christ-figure, redeeming her father.

Shows understanding of imagery and metaphor, although lacking technical vocabulary.

Meanwhile, the evil forces working in the kingdom have joined together to oppose Cordelia and her army. Goneril and Regan are more interested in fighting each other over Edmund and both end up dead. Edmund, thinking he has destroyed his brother and his father, now has his eye on the throne. To this end he bribes a captain to hang Cordelia and Lear in prison, thus removing the king and his remaining heir. Shakespeare then presents the audience with a duel between Edmund and Edgar, which diverts attention, until dying Edmund has a change of heart. Shakespeare uses the device of having a messenger exit, only for Lear to make a dramatic entrance carrying the dead Cordelia.

Shows engagement with the text and some awareness of dramatic method.

Lear tries to prove that Cordelia is not dead, fancying he sees a feather stir in her breath, but he also says he knows when one is dead and cries out, 'Why should a dog, a horse, a rat have life, / And thou no breath at all?' The motif of breathing is repeated with a memory of Cordelia's voice, with Lear's request to 'undo this button' and his dying cry to look at her lips. A.C. Bradley believes Lear dies of joy, thinking her lips have moved. Others say it is because her voice is silenced, not by Lear, as in the first scene, but by death.

Uses a relevant integrated quotation.

Makes a perceptive comment on the motif involving breath, lips, speech, but needs evaluation.

Comments on critical views, but needs more analysis and relating to own viewpoint.

This answer shows understanding and engagement with the text. There is too much narrative and not enough analysis and evaluation for the higher grades. It attempts to answer the question, but it often deviates from the main point. Perhaps more careful planning was needed to ensure that the question was being addressed.

Sample answer 3

> Explore the significance of this extract from Act 4, Scene 6, from 'Gloucester: O, let me kiss that hand!' to 'Lear: … To see the things thou dost not', with regard to the tragedy of the whole play. You should remember to analyse Shakespeare's dramatic methods.

Gives a succinct and perceptive summing up of the extract and condition of the two characters.

Makes sound analysis of the language and meaning.

Well-chosen performance example illustrates Shakespeare's dramatic methods.

This extract shows the final meeting of Gloucester and Lear, one blinded through the cruelty of Edmund, the other brought to madness by hubris and self-delusion. Their condition represents the folly of moral blindness and the wish for power without responsibility. While Gloucester, recognizing the king, wants to kiss his hand in loyalty, Lear shows his new awareness of his lack of 'addition' by saying 'it smells of mortality'. This is a scene where directors find creative ways to portray the two suffering but now morally sighted fathers revealing their insights. One director used black paint to show Gloucester's empty eye sockets and set this meeting in a blank white space for maximum effect.

Short but thoughtful evaluation of language relates to theme of nature in the play.

Good close reading and analysis of ideas links with other parts of the text.

Makes a perceptive comment about the use of humour, which is not always obvious!

Offers thoughtful analysis of sub-text and links to themes in the play.

Gloucester's reference to Lear as a 'ruin'd piece of Nature' establishes the outcast king as 'the natural man' whose basic needs make 'man's life as cheap as beast's.' For the nobleman it seems to herald the way the 'world / Shall so wear out to naught'. Lear addresses Gloucester as 'blind Cupid' which, being the sign for a brothel, suggests he has recognized him. The reference connects Gloucester back to Edmund, through whose agency he lost his eyes but also gained the protection of his legitimate son Edgar. The tragic circumstances in which this meeting takes place is not without dark humour, as Lear tells Gloucester 'Read thou this challenge' and comments 'Your eyes are in a heavy case, your purse in a light: yet you see how this world goes'. Shakespeare is using Lear's madness to show his inner perception, which is a reminder of Gloucester's own realization of Edmund's treachery and his enlightenment about Edgar's true nature.

Another of the tragic ironies in the play is Lear's belated understanding about the way in which he has governed his kingdom. From his identification with 'Poor naked wretches' in the storm, he has come to see the abuse of power that flourishes. From imagining he can keep 'th'addition of a king' without ruling, he now realizes, 'A dog's obeyed in office'. It is the power and authority of the position rather than the holder that matters. Everywhere there is power, there is corruption: 'Plate sin with gold, / And the strong lance of justice hurtless breaks; Arm it in rags, a pigmy's straw does pierce it.' The imagery of the joust, which Shakespeare's audience would have recognized, creates a metaphor for the untouchable wealthy evading justice while the poor have little chance of receiving it.

Recognizes the technique of tragic irony, supported by relevant quotation.

Uses precise quotation to illustrate a succinct point, which is then analysed briefly.

Shows sound close reading to back up views; the metaphor is well related to contextual factors.

Under the guise of madness, Lear speaks the truth he now recognizes. Hypocrisy is rife and is shown in the images of the beadle lusting after the whore and the usurer hanging the cozener. It is not hard to imagine Lear's words finding favour with the groundlings, who would recognize such situations, just as for modern audiences noting the discrepancy between e.g. those who can afford expensive accountants and those who must pay their taxes at source. The universal nature of such language is one of the reasons for the play's continuing popularity. No doubt Lear's remark 'Get thee glass eyes; / And, like a scurvy politician, seem / To see the things thou dost not' had a similar resonance for the Jacobeans as it does for audiences today.

Thoughtful ideas are supported by relevant evidence and related to universal experience as well as contextual factors.

It is tragic that these insights come too late. The evil that has been loosed by Lear's folly and Gloucester's insouciance continues right up to the end of the play and the cruel death of Cordelia. She saves Lear from the madness and suffering shown in this scene but she cannot save herself and Lear cannot save her. The evildoers all die, and so do most of the innocent, leaving only Edgar and Albany to rescue the kingdom.

Shows understanding of the notion of tragedy as fate that cannot be avoided.

These two, having witnessed the evils of a failure of kingly responsibility, should be in a better position to govern wisely. This scene shows a reconciliation and a new perception of justice, which seems to bear out Stephen Greenblatt's view of a kingship that subverts in order to reaffirm itself.

Refers to new historicist critical reading, which is relevant but needs evaluating.

Overall this is a promising answer. It makes a successful attempt to answer the question and shows a thorough understanding of Shakespeare's literary techniques and dramatic methods. There is some perceptive evaluation and analysis of themes, ideas, genre and language. The rather sketchy reference to critical theory shows awareness but needs relating to the candidate's own views.

Glossary and Further Reading

blank verse unrhymed verse; the five beats in each line are known as **iambic pentameter**

caesura a stop within the line itself, as opposed to an end-stopped line

catharsis purging of emotions created by the play, so that the audience feel restored

climax the point in a literary work in which the tension reaches its highest point

denouement the final part of the plot where all the loose ends are tied up

dramatic irony when the audience knows something that most of the characters do not

enjambment the continuation of a sentence, running one line onto the next

exposition introduction of events, settings and characters to the audience

falling action sequence of events after the climax but before the resolution

hamartia a mistake made by the protagonist, which leads to their downfall

hubris excessive or stubborn pride

iambic pentameter a rhythm; a line of five sets of syllables, each set with the stress on the second syllable, e.g. 'To **shake** all **cares** and **bus**iness **from** our **age**'

idiolect an individual person or character's way of speaking

machiavellian someone who is cunning, manipulative and deceitful; after the 15th-century political advisor Niccolo Machiavelli, who guided princes in how to maintain order and their own power by unscrupulous methods

nemesis divine retribution

peripeteia the point at which things change for the protagonist and the audience can see his or her fortunes are in decline

protagonist the main character or tragic hero

rhyming couplet two lines that rhyme on the last syllable of each

rising action series of incidents that create tension and interest for the audience

soliloquy a speech delivered by a character when they are, or believe they are, alone on stage

Books

King Lear (New Casebooks) by Professor Kiernan Ryan (Editor), Palgrave Macmillan, 1992

Shakespeare: King Lear (Casebooks Series) by Frank Kermode (Editor), Palgrave Macmillan, 1992

The Wheel of Fire by G. Wilson Knight. Routledge Classics, Taylor and Francis, 2001

Shakespearean Tragedy by A. C. Bradley, Penguin Books, 1991

Shakespeare: the Invention of the Human by Harold Bloom, Pearson Education (US), 2001

Prefaces to Shakespeare by Harley Granville-Barker, Atlantic Publishers & Distributors (P) Ltd, 2006

Shakespeare's Language by Frank Kermode, Penguin Books, 2001

Fools of Time: Studies in Shakespearean Tragedy (Alexander Lectures) by Northrop Frye, University of Toronto Press, 1996

Websites

Wordpress. King Lear: Madness and Subversion
https://literaryfocus.wordpress.com/2014/06/19/king-lear-madness-and-subversion/

RSC King Lear
https://www.rsc.org.uk/king-lear/about-the-play

National Theatre King Lear – includes several video interviews with cast and director
http://ntlive.nationaltheatre.org.uk/productions/44084-king-lear

OUP Blog: Shakespeare's Undirected Letters: Critical Confusion in King Lear
https://blog.oup.com/2008/12/shakespeares_letters/

King Lear in Performance
http://neboliterature.mrkdevelopment.com.au/drama/king-lear/lear-in-performance.html

OXFORD
UNIVERSITY PRESS

Great Clarendon Street, Oxford, OX2 6DP,
United Kingdom

Oxford University Press is a department of the University of
Oxford. It furthers the University's objective of excellence in
research, scholarship, and education by publishing worldwide.
Oxford is a registered trade mark of Oxford University Press in
the UK and in certain other countries

British Library Cataloguing in Publication Data

Data available

ISBN 978-019-839904-9

Kindle edition ISBN 978-019-839905-6

10 9 8 7 6 5 4 3 2 1

Printed in China by Leo Paper Products Ltd.

Acknowledgements

The publisher and authors would like to thank the following for
permission to use photographs and other copyright material:

Cover: © Drunaa/Trevillion Images; **p6:** Everett Collection Inc/
Alamy Stock Photo; **p10:** Geraint Lewis/Alamy Stock Photo;
p14: Wikimedia Commons/Public Domain; **p17:** REUTERS/
Alamy Stock Photo; **p20:** GL Archive/Alamy Stock Photo; **p23:**
Pictorial Press Ltd/Alamy Stock Photo; **p26:** 1 Collection/Alamy
Stock Photo; **p28:** Travelshots/Superstock; **p34:** Photo by Ellie
Kurttz © RSC; **p36:** Reg Wilson/REX/Shutterstock; **p45:** Geraint
Lewis/REX/Shutterstock; **p48:** Robbie Jack - Corbis/Getty Images;
p51: Photo by Ellie Kurttz © RSC; **p56:** Everett Collection Inc/
Alamy Stock Photo; **p61:** Photo by Ellie Kurttz © RSC; **p64:** ITV/
REX/Shutterstock; **p66:** Donald Cooper/REX/Shutterstock; **p73:**
ITV/REX/Shutterstock; **p76:** Nigel R. Barklie/REX/Shutterstock;
p79: Moviestore collection Ltd/Alamy Stock Photo; **p81:**
Geraint Lewis/Alamy Stock Photo; **p85:** Alastair Muir/REX/
Shutterstock; **p89:** Geraint Lewis/Alamy Stock Photo; **p92:** Ray
Tang/REX/Shutterstock.

Extracts are from William Shakespeare: King Lear, Oxford
School Shakespeare edited by Roma Gill (OUP, 2012)

We are grateful for permission to reprint the following
copyright texts:

Joseph Carroll: extract from *An Evolutionary Approach
to Shakespeare's King Lear* (Great Neck Publishing, 2012),
reprinted by permission of the author.

David Chandler: extract from 'The Essence of
Shakespearean Tragedy', copyright © David Chandler 1984,
in *King Lear: Critical Essays* edited by Kenneth Muir (Routledge,
2015), reprinted by permission of the author.

Philip Collington: extract from 'Self-Discovery in
Montaigne's 'Of Solitarinesse' and King Lear ' in *Comparative
Drama*, Vol 35, Numbers 3.4 (2001-2002), reprinted by
permission of the author.

Barbara Everett: extract from 'The New King Lear', *The
Critical Quarterly*, Dec 1960, reprinted by permission of
Blackwell Publishing Ltd via Copyright Clearance Center, Inc.

Coppelia Kahn: extract from 'The Absent Mother in *King
Lear*' first published in *Rewriting the Rennaissance: The Discourse
of Sexual Differences in Early Modern Europe* edited by Margaret
W Ferguson, Maureen Quilligan and Nancy J Vickers
(University of Chicago Press, 1986), reprinted permission of
the author and the publishers.

G Wilson Knight: extracts from *The Wheel of Fire: Essays on
interpretation of Shakespeare's tragedy* (2e, Routledge, 2005),
copyright © G Wilson Knight 1930, reprinted by permission
of Taylor & Francis Books, UK.

Lesley Kordecki and Karla Koskinen: extract from
introduction to *Revisioning Lear's Daughters* (Palgrave
Macmillan, 2010), copyright © Lesley Kordecki and Karla
Koskinen 2010, reprinted by permission of Springer Nature.

Kathleeen McLuskie: extract from 'The Patriarchal
Bard: Feminist Criticism and Shakespeare: King Lear and
Measure for Measure' in *Political Shakespeare: essays in cultural
materialism* edited by J Dollimore and A Sinfield (Manchester
University Press, 1994), reprinted by permission of the
publishers.

Kenneth Muir: extracts from introduction to the Arden
Shakespeare *King Lear* (Methuen 1952), copyright © Kenneth
Muir 1952, reprinted by permission of the publishers,
Bloomsbury Arden Shakespeare, an imprint of Bloomsbury
Publishing Plc.

C J Sisson: extracts from *Shakespeare's Tragic Justice*
(Methuen, 1963/ Routledge, 2017), reprinted by permission of
the Taylor & Francis Group.

J Stampfer: extract from 'The Catharsis of King Lear' in
Shakespeare Survey 13 edited by Allardyce Nicholl (Cambridge,
1960), reprinted by permission of Cambridge University
Press

Kenneth Tynan: extract from review 'Paul Scofield
and Peter Brook's *King Lear*', *The Observer*, 11 Nov 1962,
republished 24 Jan 2014 theguardian.com, copyright ©
Guardian News & Media Ltd 2014, reprinted by permission
of GNM.

David Walsh: extract from a review of *King Lear*, World
Socialist Web Site, 21st Nov 2002, reprinted by permission of
the author.

We have made every effort to trace and contact copyright
holders before publication. If notified, the publisher will
rectify any errors or omissions at the earliest opportunity.